NIGHT SKY
IDENTIFIER

NIGHT SKY
I D E N T I F I E R

MALLARD PRESS

Dedication
To Alison and Elizabeth

MALLARD PRESS
An imprint of BDD Promotional
Book Company, Inc.,
666 Fifth Avenue
New York, NY 10103

Mallard Press and its accompanying design
and logo are trademarks of
BDD Promotional Book Company, Inc.

First published in the United States of America
in 1992 by the Mallard Press

ISBN 0–7924–5520–7

This book was designed and produced by
Quintet Publishing Limited
6 Blundell Street
London N7 9BH

Creative Director: Terry Jeavons
Designer: Chris Dymond
Project Editor: Sally Harper
Editor: Amanda Ronan

Typeset in Great Britain by
Central Southern Typesetters, Eastbourne
Manufactured in Singapore by
Chroma Graphics (Overseas) PTE Ltd
Printed in Hong Kong by
Leefung-Asco Printers Limited

Contents

Introduction

*T*he vast cosmos in which we live contains everything that has ever been, is, or ever will be. The planet upon which we live, and the Solar System of which our speck of a world is a part, fade into insignificance when compared with the universe as a whole.

From our vantage point on Earth we are able to peer out into the gulf of space; telescopes reveal a whole host of celestial objects scattered throughout its limitless depths. The Solar System, our own cosmic backyard, contains the Sun, the star which provides us with light and heat and permits the existence of life on the Earth. There are also nine major planets, each one different in many ways to its neighbours, together with the asteroids, comets and shooting stars, the latter revealing themselves as ghostly

A B O V E: *Rich starfields around the constellations Cygnus, Cepheus and Lacerta. The Milky Way can be clearly seen passing through this region.*

streaks of light crossing the starlit sky. The occasional near miss of an Earth-grazing asteroid, or the impact of meteorites, reminds us that the universe is indeed on our doorstep.

Beyond the Solar System are the stars, huge balls of incandescent gas that pour out energy into surrounding space. Many of these stars are immensely more powerful than our own Sun, and only appear as tiny points of light because of their huge distances from us.

Although some stars are solitary suns in space, many are members of double, triple and multiple systems, or of the much grander collections of stars we call star clusters. Often we see such clusters lying within or near nebulae, huge interstellar clouds of gas and dust that reveal themselves to our gaze either by reflecting

L E F T: *Area of sky around Musca. The brightest stars within the constellation form a prominent (but somewhat lop-sided) quadrilateral at the centre of the picture, while Acrux (Alpha Crucis) is seen at top left.*

the light from nearby stars, or by absorbing colossal amounts of energy from suns embedded within them and in turn giving off the visible light that registers on the inquisitive eyes of the astronomer.

All these objects, and more, are found within the boundaries of our own Galaxy. Other galaxies, scattered throughout space, are home to similar collections of celestial objects. The galaxies themselves are often huge systems, the sizes of which sometimes stretch the imagination. A ray of light, travelling at the colossal speed of 186,000 miles (300,000km) per second, would take around 100,000 years to cross from one edge of our Galaxy to the other! Some galaxies are even larger, and the distances between so-called 'neighbouring' galaxies dwarf even these huge figures. Professional astronomers have detected the pale glow of objects which are so far away from us that the light we are seeing today set off towards us over twice the age of the Solar System ago! (See page 28 for explanation of 'light-years'.) When we consider that our Sun and family of planets came into being somewhere in the region of 5,000 million years or so ago, the true immensity of the universe really starts to come home to us!

Yet it is virtually impossible to even try and imagine these huge distances. After all, there are few who could identify with the 250,000 miles (400,000km) or so that the Apollo astronauts crossed to reach the Moon, our closest neighbour in space. Yet this inability is natural and will not in any way spoil our enjoyment of the starry sky.

There are many different objects in the heavens that are within the light grasp of small telescopes, binoculars or even the naked eye. It is simply a case of knowing where to look and what to expect to see when you find the object you seek. The visually stunning images captured by the world's large telescopes do, it is true, lead some to expect a similar sight when viewing the same object from their own backyard. Yet this is seldom the case. The star clusters, nebulae and galaxies within our visual reach quite often appear as nothing more than diffuse patches of light. However, the more time you spend observing, the more detail your eyes will be able to pick out from the view presented through even the moderate optical equipment owned by most amateurs. In other words, practice makes perfect, and you actually *learn* to see!

Initially, much of the fun in being a backyard astronomer is to actually track down the objects you wish to observe. The star charts included in this book, together with the hints given will help you to locate a wealth of different objects, some easier to pick out than others. Take your time in searching for them, don't give up if you don't succeed straight away and persevere until you finally identify what it is you are searching for. The rewards, as you will see, can be great. Happy stargazing!

B E L O W: *Regulus (Alpha Leonis), the brightest star in Leo and the 21st brightest star in the sky.*

Looking at the Sky

Binoculars

Although many types of observation require the use of a telescope, a large number of amateur astronomers use binoculars as their first choice of observing instrument. They are an extremely versatile and portable low-cost instrument and their uses spread well beyond the borders of astronomy. Binoculars open many doors on the Universe: they can reveal a host of lunar features, and their wide fields of view enable the faint glows from many star clusters and other deep sky objects to be detected. They are also ideally suited to the observation of variable stars, a great number of which remain within the light grasp of binoculars throughout their entire period of variability. Many a discoverer of comets or novae also owe their achievements to the use of binoculars.

Binoculars are comfortable to use, enabling observation to be carried out with both eyes simultaneously, unlike conventional telescopes which may involve long periods of observation with one eye only.

BELOW: The folded light paths of prismatic binoculars give them their characteristic bulky shape.

CHOOSING AND BUYING BINOCULARS

Binoculars are classified by a pair of numbers, such as 12×50 or 7×50, the first denoting the magnification and the second the diameter of the object glasses (aperture) in millimetres. Ideally, the largest magnification for hand-held binoculars is 7×, anything larger than this giving a correspondingly narrower field of view, thereby making the binoculars difficult to keep trained on the object being observed for prolonged periods. However, this depends on the individual, and 10× or even 12× may be fine for some people. Although magnification is important, aperture should really be the main consideration when buying binoculars (or telescopes). The light-gathering power of instruments with a 3.2in (80mm) aperture will far exceed those of, say, 2in (50mm) aperture. The larger instrument will therefore be capable of detecting fainter objects. As with any optical equipment, binoculars should make use of all available light. Therefore the size of exit pupil is all important. The exit pupil is the image formed by the eyepiece, its diameter being calculated by dividing the magnification into the object glass diameter. The maximum diameter of the fully dark-adapted eye pupil is around 0.3in (7mm), so a similar-sized exit pupil would be ideal and would fully utilize the image delivered by the binoculars. A pair of 7×50 binoculars would produce a 50/7 = 0.3in (7mm) exit pupil, as well as being light and easy to hold, providing good magnification and having excellent light-gathering power. Binoculars of this size are considered best for general observation.

Camera and photographic shops, astronomical equipment suppliers, department stores, mail order catalogues ... the list of potential sources for binoculars is almost endless. However, because you should really see what you are buying before you part with your money, do not consider mail order unless there is a guarantee of getting your money back in the event of faulty or substandard goods.

You can save money by purchasing second-hand binoculars, although these must have been well maintained by their previous owner. A general

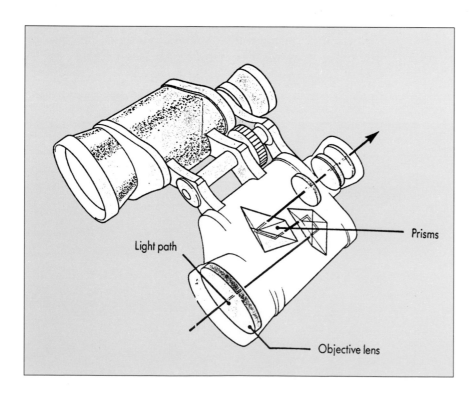

Light path

Prisms

Objective lens

inspection for dents or other damage to the binocular body should be carried out. Any such damage, if found, may indicate further unseen faults inside the instrument. The overall standard of workmanship should be as high as possible. Check that the central pivot (around which the binoculars are adjusted to bring the eyepieces in line with your eyes) operates firmly but smoothly and isn't slack in any way. Also check out the focusing mechanism; the eyepiece barrels should run in and out smoothly with no sideways play, and should remain at the point of focus when set. They should also be firm even when extended fully.

Check the exit pupils by holding the binoculars in the viewing position, but away from your eyes. The exit pupils will appear as discs of light in the eyepieces. The discs should be complete, 'squared-off' edges to the discs showing that the prisms inside the binoculars are not allowing all the available light through to the eyepieces.

Check carefully that the barrels are set parallel to each other. If not, a double image will result. Open and close your eyes while looking repeatedly through the binoculars. Although your eyes will automatically compensate for any double image, this would almost certainly result in eye strain or headaches if prolonged. Carefully examining the binoculars this way will reveal any double image prior to your eyes adjusting. Discard any binoculars that display this fault.

The objective glasses of the vast majority of binoculars and telescopes have anti-reflection coatings. Any equipment without such a coating should not be purchased. These coatings are there to improve contrast and the light transmission of the optical system.

ABOVE: *Splendid wide-field views of the Milky Way can be obtained with binoculars. Sweeping the Milky Way in areas such as that around Cassiopeia and Perseus, seen here, will reveal many rich starfields.*

BELOW: *Binoculars are ideal for observing the principal lunar features. Many of the dark maria and larger craters are within reach of binoculars.*

Although many binoculars are presented as being 'fully coated' this is often not the case, such coatings often being restricted to the outer surfaces of object glass and eyepiece glass only! A coated surface will produce a coloured reflection of a bright light source, such as a strip light. If you stand with your back to a light source and suitably position the binoculars, you will see a pair of reflections in the main object glass, these being from the front and back of the lens. Coloured reflection(s) indicate coated surfaces, and at least one surface should be coated. The eyepiece lenses can also be tested in this way.

Finally, be patient, and do not buy the first pair of binoculars you see. Check them over carefully before parting with your money, and remember that they will be accompanying you on your many observing sessions. Make sure that you get a useful astronomical instrument, and not a liability . . .

BINOCULAR ACCESSORIES
Camera tripods are suitable for holding large binoculars, or those with high magnifications, steady during use. Binocular adaptors are available which allow you to clamp the binoculars to the tripod head. Tall tripods are preferred, equipped with a head that can be adjusted to allow for viewing at awkward angles. Insist on a full set of protective lens caps, a sturdy carrying case and a carrying strap. The latter should be worn *at all times* when using the binoculars. This is a wise precaution. Not only will you feel silly if you drop the binoculars; they can also be expensive to replace!

Telescopes

Telescopes are expensive and, although the first reaction of many budding and enthusiastic backyard astronomers is to go out and purchase one straight away, this should only be after a reasonably thorough working knowledge of the night sky has been achieved through observation both with the naked eye and through binoculars.

As with binoculars, the light-gathering power of a telescope is governed by the diameter of the main lens or mirror. The larger the diameter, the greater the area available to collect light. This results in brighter images and, consequently, the ability to pick up fainter objects. Because astronomy is all about the observation of faint objects, aperture is one of the main considerations when purchasing a telescope.

Whatever instrument is chosen, ignore claims of high magnifications made by some manufacturers. The limit of *useful* magnification depends upon the amount of light available. The higher the magnification, the smaller the field of view and, consequently, the lower the amount of available light. In order to optimize high magnifications, large apertures are needed to gather the limited amount of light that is available. A magnification of 600× would

be absolutely useless with a telescope of only 2.5in (60mm) aperture. To make use of such magnification a much larger objective would be needed.

Each telescope has a *maximum useful magnification* and this information should be displayed with any commercially available telescope. As a general guide, the maximum useful magnification for small telescopes is roughly equal to 50× per 1in (25mm) of aperture. In other words, for a 2.5in (60mm) aperture telescope a magnification of 600× would be useless, the maximum useful magnification being 125×. The maximum useful magnification for a 4in (100mm) instrument is 200× and so on.

TYPES OF TELESCOPES

There are two main types of telescope: refractors and reflectors. Refractors use a lens to collect light from the object being observed while reflectors use a specially shaped mirror. In each case, the light is brought to a focus at a distance from the main lens (or mirror) known as the focal length. Here, the resulting image is magnified by a second lens known as an eyepiece. Telescopes usually come complete with several different eyepieces to give a range of magnifications. The actual magnification delivered by an eyepiece is calculated by dividing its focal length in-

BELOW: *Professional astronomers have access to very large telescopes, such as the 4-metre Mayall Telescope at Kitt Peak National Observatory in Arizona.*

LEFT: *Even a small telescope will reveal the rings of Saturn.*

mum useful apertures are around 3in (76mm) for a refractor and 6in (152mm) for a reflector, although beginners can start out with either a 2.5in (60mm) refractor or 4.5in (112mm) reflector.

Generally speaking, refractors are more effective than reflectors, offering better resolution of fine detail and making them ideal for the observation of double stars, planets, the Moon and so on. However, reflectors usually offer a wider field of view making them much more suited to the study of star clusters, nebulae and galaxies. Refractors are also generally more robust than reflectors, their optical systems staying aligned during normal transportation and handling. Reflectors are not as sturdy and require periodic maintenance and realigning of the optical components.

to that of the telescope. In other words, an eyepiece of 0.5in (12mm) focal length, when used with a telescope of focal length 36in (900mm), will give a magnification of 900/12, or 75×.

Refractors suffer from false colour (chromatic aberration), in that the different wavelengths of light (light itself is a blend of all colours of the spectrum from long wavelength red through to short wavelength blue) are brought to focus at different points. Light passing through the objective is bent, or refracted, to a focus. However, longer wavelengths are bent less sharply than shorter ones, resulting in the different wavelengths being brought to focus at different points. Achromatic lenses can partly cure the problems of chromatic aberration. These lenses contain two components, each of which is made from a different type of glass. As the light passes through both components, the amount of false colour is reduced somewhat as the errors largely cancel each other out. Because mirrors reflect all colours equally and don't spread out light of different wavelengths, there is no chromatic aberration. However, some false colour may be produced in the eyepiece.

Aperture for aperture, a refractor is more expensive than a reflector. This is a direct result of the work required to produce an achromatic lens, each component of which has two surfaces to figure unlike mirrors, which have a single reflecting surface. Mini-

RIGHT: *Small telescopes will reveal the broad equatorial cloud belts of Jupiter together with its four largest moons, some of which are seen here.*

TELESCOPE MOUNTINGS

All telescopes should have mountings to hold them steady during use. Bad, unsturdy mountings produce telescope 'shake' and, consequently, bad performance from even the best optics.

For small telescopes altitude-azimuth (alt-azimuth) mounts are commonly used. These allow the instrument to be moved both vertically (altitude) and horizontally (azimuth). The alt-azimuth mounting is fine for casual or wide-field stargazing, although unsuitable for many areas of serious work. The rising and setting of stars due to the Earth's rotation causes their positions in the sky to constantly change in altitude and azimuth. In order to keep the object under observation in the field of view, an alt-azimuth mount must therefore be constantly adjusted in two axes.

To overcome this problem, equatorial mountings are used. These can be aligned with the Earth's axis, and enable the object being studied to be kept in the field of view by adjustment of one axis only, this adjustment often being carried out with an automatic clockwork or electric drive mechanism.

The Solar System

The Sun

Although the Sun is the brightest and most visually accessible object in the sky, in reality it is just another star, only appearing so bright because it lies so close to us. The extremely high temperature and pressure at the Sun's core give rise to thermonuclear reactions which produce energy. During these reactions, hydrogen is being converted to helium. A tiny percentage of mass is left over. After slowly making its way to the solar surface it escapes into space as light and heat.

The yellow, visible surface of the Sun that we see is called the photosphere, and there are many features visible both on and above it. These include sunspots, which are cooler areas of the photosphere and which appear as dark patches against the surrounding, brighter surface. Sunspots are associated with the strong, solar magnetic field. They can appear either singly or in groups, and can last anything from a few days to several weeks. A sunspot can be seen to cross the visible disc of the Sun over a period of several days, thus displaying the Sun's axial rotation. The Sun takes roughly a month to make one full rotation.

Huge jets of hot gas can sometimes be seen above the photosphere. These so-called prominences are of two basic types. Eruptive prominences change rapidly and are formed as gas is lifted away from the Sun at speeds of up to several hundred miles per second. Quiescent prominences are much more docile and can hang above the solar surface for many weeks or months on end.

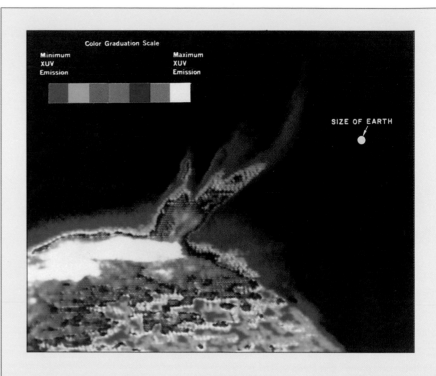

A B O V E: *Photograph of a solar eruption taken by astronauts on the Skylab mission in August 1973.*

OBSERVING THE SUN

On no account must you ever look directly at the Sun either with the naked eye or through a telescope or binoculars, as permanent damage to your eyes could result. By far the safest way to observe the Sun is by image projection. This involves the projection of an image of the Sun through the telescope and onto a screen. The entire solar disc can be seen at one go when projection

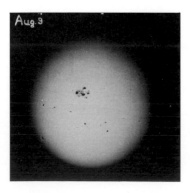

Mercury

Mercury is the closest planet to the Sun and one of the four inner, terrestrial planets, bodies similar to the Earth in composition, being made up primarily of rock and metallic materials with little if any hydrogen, helium or other gas present.

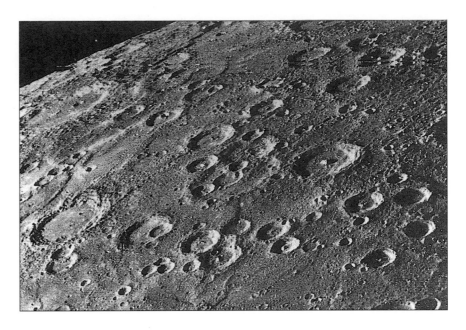

ABOVE: *The crater-strewn surface of Mercury revealed by the cameras of the Mariner 10 probe.*

is carried out through a low-power eyepiece. Higher power eyepieces enable enlarged and more detailed images of selected areas of the solar disc to be obtained.

Sunspots are the easiest type of solar feature to observe. They are seen to have a dark, central area, known as the umbra, surrounded by a lighter penumbra. Sunspot activity varies throughout the 11-year solar cycle, a definite period of sunspot activity first noted by Heinrich Schwabe in 1843. On days around minimum activity you may find the Sun totally devoid of spots for several days or even weeks at a time. However, at its maximum the solar disc may be swarming with active areas.

Faculae are seen as bright patches of light against the photosphere. These bright clouds of hydrogen are similar in brightness to the photosphere and offer little contrast when seen near the centre of the solar disc. Near the limb (the apparent edge of the Sun), however, they are far more prominent as their light originates in the chromosphere several hundred miles above the photosphere. If you see faculae, keep an eye on the area in question as they tend to appear in potential sunspot areas, and an active sunspot group may well be on the way!

FACING PAGE BELOW: *Four photographs of the solar disc taken between 7 and 13 August 1917, showing the rotation of the Sun.*

BELOW: *Topographic map of the Venusian surface obtained during the American Pioneer-Venus radar mapping mission.*

the Caloris basin, a huge formation some 813 miles (1,300km) across and bordered by mountains rising up to 1.2 miles (2km) above the Mercurian surface.

Venus

Venus appears to be the brightest planet in the sky because it is completely covered by dense, white clouds which reflect sunlight extremely well but completely hide the surface from view. It is only recently that space probes using special radar mapping techniques have given us an idea as to what the surface of Venus looks like. Much of the surface area is made up of flat rolling plains, although there are numerous craters, valleys and possibly active volcanoes. There are also several highland regions, the largest of which are Ishtar Terra, in the Venusian northern hemisphere, and Aphrodite Terra, which straddles the equator.

Mercury is seen near the Sun in the sky, either low down in the west after sunset or in the east before sunrise, and astronomers have always had difficulty observing the planet. It was not until the mid-1970s that the American Mariner 10 probe sent back the first really good pictures of its surface.

Mariner 10 revealed a planet pitted with craters, rather like the Moon, although there were few of the dark plains we associate with the lunar surface. The most impressive feature observed by Mariner 10 was

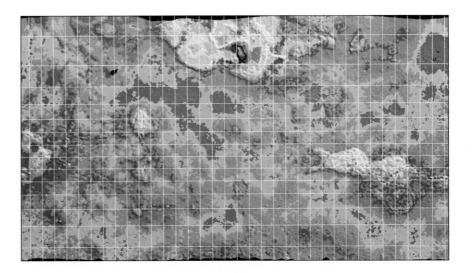

Mars

Mars is often referred to as the Red Planet, its surface playing host to vast areas of reddish dust which give rise to the planet's strong reddish hue. Occasionally all or part of the Martian surface may be hidden from view, for days or even weeks on end, as Martian winds whip up dust from the surface to produce a screen that effectively blocks our view of the planet.

The American Mariner missions, during the 1960s and early 1970s, gave us our first clear views of the Martian surface. These were supplemented by the American Viking probes. Consisting of both orbiters and landers, Viking 1 and 2 sent back many thousands of pictures of Mars from orbit together with photographs and measurements taken from the surface by the two landers.

Mars has a wide diversity of surface features including craters, valleys and volcanoes. Vallis Marineris is a huge valley system, 375 miles (600km) wide in places and stretching for a full 2,800 miles (4,500km) around the Martian equatorial regions. Equally im-

ABOVE *The first colour photograph of the Martian surface taken by the Viking 1 lander in July 1976.*

pressive is Olympus Mons, a huge 16 mile (25km) high volcano which totally dwarfs even the largest Earth volcanoes. Olympus Mons measures around 375 miles (600km) across at its base and has a caldera 50 miles (80km) across.

OBSERVING THE TERRESTRIAL PLANETS

Both Mercury and Venus are quite bright. Consequently, the faint and somewhat obscure details glimpsed on their discs can easily be lost in their glare if they are observed against a dark sky. They are seen to best advantage when viewed against a comparatively bright sky, although great care must be taken when doing this. Damage to your eyesight may result through casually sweeping the region of sky containing either of these objects during daylight hours if the Sun is accidentally brought into the field of view. Daytime observation should only be carried out by experienced observers.

Both Mercury and Venus display phases, similar to those of the Moon. Magnifications of around 150× will show the Mercurian phases, which change quickly because of Mercury's rapid orbital motion. The phases of Venus are easily seen with magnifications of only around 50× or so. Markings in the Venusian atmosphere have been detected, although these are very difficult to make out.

RIGHT: *Their proximity to the Sun means that Mercury and Venus are seen either in the east before sunrise or in the west after sunset. This view show Venus (lower left) and Mercury in the sunset sky in March 1978.*

When Mars is suitably placed, surface features, comprised of material with a comparatively low reflectivity, or albedo, may often be seen through instruments of only 4in (100mm) aperture, although telescopes of at least twice this aperture are needed for serious observation of the planet. There are quite a number of these so-called albedo features, good examples of which are the prominent V-shaped Syrtis Major, located in the Martian equatorial region, and Mare Acidalium, found in the northern hemisphere. Localized dust storms may occasionally be seen as yellowish patches above the Martian surface.

The Minor Planets

These are tiny planetary objects, most of which orbit the Sun between Mars and Jupiter. The first to be discovered was Ceres, spotted by Giuseppe Piazzi in 1801. The next three – Pallas, Juno and Vesta – came to light in 1802, 1804 and 1807 respectively, after which no more were found until 1845, when Karl Hencke located Astraea. Since then, discoveries have been made every year. It is thought that the minor planets are actually debris, left over after the Solar System was formed. All are small by planetary standards, the largest, Ceres, being only around 625 miles (1,000km) in diameter. Some minor planets have diameters of less than a mile, although there must be many more, as yet undetected, that are even smaller.

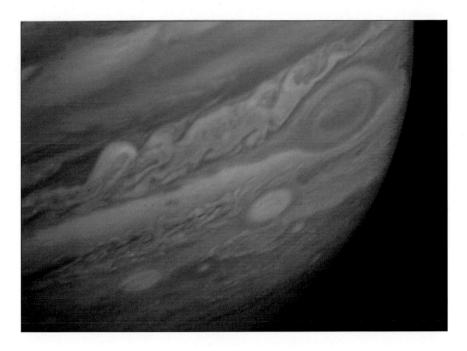

ABOVE: *A spectacular photograph taken by Voyager 2 showing a disturbed region to the west of the Great Red Spot.*

BELOW RIGHT: *This Voyager photograph shows the vivid surface colouration resulting from Io's extensive volcanic activity.*

OBSERVING THE MINOR PLANETS

The minor planets are also known as the asteroids, meaning 'starlike', a name indicative of their appearance even through large telescopes. A pair of good binoculars or a small telescope will easily pick up the four largest asteroids – Ceres, Pallas, Juno and Vesta – when suitably placed. Vesta can be glimpsed with the naked eye under exceptional observing conditions, although thorough dark adaptation, and a knowledge of exactly where to look, are essential.

Asteroids give themselves away by their movement across the sky. To identify an asteroid, positional details are needed. By drawing stars seen in the same telescopic field as the asteroid, and doing a similar drawing a night or two later, one of the 'stars' will, hopefully, be seen to have moved against the background stars!

The dark belts and brighter zones seen crossing the Jovian disc are regions of tremendous activity. Gas welling up from the Jovian interior to cool at the surface forms the lighter zones, while the belts are regions where the gas is descending out of view.

An interesting feature to be seen on Jupiter is the Great Red Spot, first observed by Giovanni Cassini in 1665 and seen almost continuously ever since. The size of the Great Red Spot varies, sometimes reaching a length of 25,000 miles (40,000km), equivalent to three times the Earth's diameter!

Jupiter has an extensive satellite family, the four largest of which were discovered in 1610 by Galileo. Known as the Galilean satellites, space probes have revealed them to be fascinating worlds. Heavy cratering peppers the surfaces of Ganymede and Callisto, while Europa is covered by a thick layer of water ice. Io is perhaps one of the most fascinating objects in the Solar System, playing host to almost continuous volcanic activity.

Jupiter

Jupiter is an impressive sight through Earth-based telescopes, its swirling atmosphere offering much to the observer. It is the largest of the planets and, like the other gas giants (Saturn, Uranus and Neptune), is comprised mainly of hydrogen and helium and does not have a solid surface.

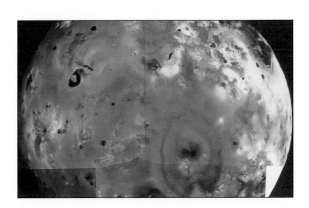

Saturn

Like Jupiter, Saturn's disc displays alternating zones and belts, although these are far less colourful or prominent than those of Jupiter. However, what Saturn lacks in visual splendour is more than compensated for in its impressive ring system, described by many sky-watchers as the most stunning telescopic sight in the heavens.

Girdling the Saturnian equator, the rings are made up of countless tiny particles that range in diameter from just a few microns to several metres. From Earth we can make out several main sections to the rings; the brightest ring B, the somewhat fainter ring A and the dim ring C, also called the Crepe Ring. Two divisions in the rings are evident; the Cassini Division separating the A and B rings, and the Encke Division, located within the A ring.

Space probes have shown us that the main ring sections are formed from countless narrow ringlets, some of which are seen within the Cassini Divison. Further rings have also been observed; an innermost D ring, located inside the Crepe Ring, and the outermost F, G and E rings.

Saturn has the most extensive satellite family in the Solar System, the largest member of which is Titan. Space probes have shown that Titan is enveloped in an opaque, reddish-orange atmosphere, comprised mainly of nitrogen, which completely hides its surface from view. For the time being, the nature of Titan remains somewhat mysterious.

ABOVE RIGHT: *Colour variations in this Voyager photo indicate different chemical composition in Saturn's rings.*

ABOVE LEFT: *Image of Saturn assembled from Voyager 2 images obtained on 4 August 1981 from 21 million km (13 million miles). Three of Saturn's moons are visible: (from left) Rhea, Diane and Tethys.*

OBSERVING JUPITER AND SATURN

Even small telescopes will show the Jovian belts and zones and, given suitable observing conditions, these may display individual features and irregularities. Telescopes of at least 6in (150mm) diameter will be needed to show the Great Red Spot.

The four Galilean satellites are all large and bright enough to be observable through binoculars or a small telescope, their motions around the planet being apparent even over fairly short periods. The satellites can sometimes be seen to cross the disc of Jupiter or to pass behind it.

Saturn's major features (the disc, main rings and Titan) can be resolved with telescopes of just 2.5in (60mm) aperture, although larger instruments are needed for detailed studies. Saturn's ring system is the most visually dramatic aspect of the planet. Although the A and B rings can be seen with small telescopes, larger instruments are needed to pick out the C ring and the Cassini and Encke Divisions.

The Earth passes through Saturn's equatorial plane twice during the planet's 29-year orbital period, at which times the rings are placed edge-on and become extremely difficult to see. When exactly aligned with Earth they may disappear from view altogether.

The brightest satellite, Titan, can be seen through good binoculars or a small telescope, although most of the other satellites are beyond the range of amateur telescopes. Titan can be followed from night to night as it travels in its 16-day orbit around Saturn.

Uranus

Discovered by William Herschel in 1781, Uranus was the first planet to be discovered with the use of a telescope. One of the most unusual things about the planet is its large axial tilt. This amounts to almost 98°, and puts its polar regions close to the plane of its orbit around the Sun. At certain times in its orbit the Sun shines down on the Uranian equator, whilst the poles are also alternately presented to the Sun. Needless to say, this phenomenon produces unusual seasonal effects on the planet!

Uranus has a total of 15 known satellites: the largest is Titania, the surface of which has been seen to contain many craters, ice cliffs and valleys. Uranus also has a ring system, first brought to light in 1977 when the planet occulted, or passed in front of, a star. The light from the star was seen to fade several times both before and after it passed behind Uranus, leading astronomers to the conclusion that a ring system girdled the planet.

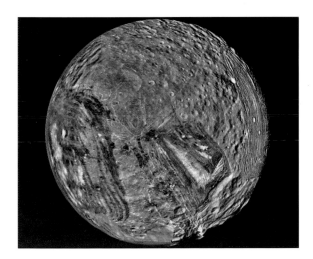

Neptune

Discovered by Johann Galle and Heinrich D'Arrest in 1846, Neptune is visible through large telescopes as a pale-bluish disc. The Voyager 2 cameras showed a variety of atmospheric features when it passed the planet in 1989. These include bright polar collars and bands of blue girdling the southern hemisphere. Cirrus clouds were also seen some 30 miles (50km) above the main cloud deck. Some dark features were seen, notably the Great Dark Spot, located around 22° south of the Neptunian equator. This feature was revealed as a hole in the Neptunian clouds, which allowed us to see to greater depths of the atmosphere.

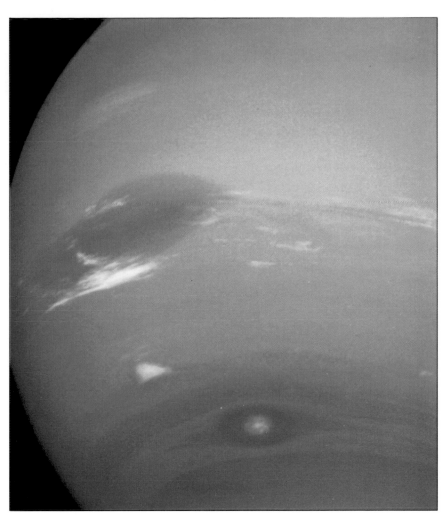

ABOVE: *Voyager 2 image of Neptune with the Great Dark Spot prominent near Neptune's limb. The similar, but much smaller Dark Spot 2 is visible near bottom of picture.*

LEFT: *This Voyager 2 picture of Miranda, the smallest of the previously known satellites of Uranus, shows many different features. An area of ancient, cratered landscape contrasts with grooved terrain of valleys and ridges.*

Neptune has a total of eight satellites all of which, apart from Triton and Nereid, were discovered by Voyager 2. The same cameras also revealed a number of faint rings girdling the planet, thereby showing that all four of the gas giant planets possessed ring systems.

Pluto

Pluto is the smallest planet in the Solar System, and the most recent to be discovered. It also has the most eccentric orbit of any planet. For 20 years of its 248-year journey around the Sun, Pluto actually comes inside the orbital path of Neptune, thereby temporarily giving up its role as the outermost planet. Pluto has one satellite, Charon, discovered in 1978. It has been found to be roughly half the size of Pluto itself, leading astronomers to regard the Pluto-Charon system as a double planet, rather than a planet and satellite.

Pluto is so far away that we know little if anything about conditions there. It is thought to consist primarily of frozen methane, although this is only educated guesswork.

OBSERVING THE OUTER PLANETS

Identifying Uranus, Neptune or Pluto is a challenge to the observer. Unlike the asteroids, the outer planets move much more slowly across the sky and their motions against the background stars will be apparent only over a few nights.

Of the three outer planets, only Uranus ever becomes bright enough to be visible to the unaided eye. Telescopically, it displays a greenish disc, upon which various features may be glimpsed by a keen-eyed observer under good viewing conditions. However, these are very difficult to see, and nowhere near as impressive as the swirling cloud belts of Jupiter or even the dusky markings of Saturn. All the Uranian satellites are out of reach of most amateur telescopes, Titania itself only reaching magnitude 14 at best.

Appearing as a bluish disc in telescopes, Neptune is much harder to spot than Uranus. Generally, Neptune will show no detail on its tiny disc, although a number of astronomers have claimed sightings of features in its clouds. However, these observers were using telescopes that would normally be unavailable to the amateur.

Although both Uranus and Neptune can be spotted through binoculars or a small telescope, Pluto is considerably fainter, and can only be seen in large telescopes. Most amateur astronomers have never observed Pluto, and the positive identification of this tiny little world can be regarded as a notable achievement!

Comets

A huge cloud of material is believed to surround the Solar System. Stretching out from beyond the orbit of Pluto to a distance of some two light-years, this cloud is believed to be formed from clumps of icy material left over from the formation of the Sun and planets. Comets are thought to originate from within this cloud of matter.

As the clump nears the Sun, solar energy acts upon it. The ice within the clump is vaporized, releasing a cloud of material which envelops what will become the cometary nucleus.

This cloud is known as the coma and it too is acted upon by relentless solar pressure. Material is pushed away from the coma, usually to form two tails: a dust tail and an ion tail, the latter formed of ionized atoms (that is, atoms that have lost one or more electrons).

As a comet rounds the Sun and begins to move away again, the effects of solar energy decrease. The tails gradually disappear, followed by the coma. Eventually, only the icy nucleus is left to continue its journey around the Solar System.

Although some comets take a few years to orbit the Sun, others take much longer. The shortest known orbital period for a comet is that of Encke's Comet, which takes just 3.3 years to travel once around the Sun. Halley's Comet takes 76 years, while others take much longer still. Some comets have orbits that are so long that astronomers are unable to measure them accurately.

ABOVE: *Discovered in November 1975 by Richard M West, Comet West made a spectacular appearance in the pr-sunrise skies of March 1976.*

LEFT: *The Voyager 2 cameras look back at Neptune's two brightest rings, the particles within them scattering sunlight back to the watching spacecraft.*

OBSERVING COMETS

Details of forthcoming returns of periodic comets are given in many astronomical publications, and these can be used to help you search for and locate them. Comets give themselves away by their distinctly diffuse and unstarlike appearance when viewed through a telescope or binoculars.

Once a comet comes into view, regular observation will show its motion through the sky. Wide field telescopes will help reveal details in the tail, while higher magnifications may reveal various features in and around the coma.

Occasionally, particles may enter the atmosphere which are large enough to at least partially survive the journey to the Earth's surface. These objects are called meteorites and many examples of them have been found. There are three main types; iron meteorites, stony meteorites (the most common) and stony-iron meteorites (the rarest group); each of these is further divided into smaller groups.

Luckily, large meteorite falls are rare, although when they do occur a great deal of damage can be caused. Meteorite craters have been found across the globe, the most famous of which is the Arizona Meteorite Crater. The study of meteorites has led astronomers to the conclusion that many originate within the asteroid belt, arising from collisions between larger bodies.

Meteors

Millions of tiny particles of dust, or meteoroids, orbit the Sun, rather like tiny planets. Occasionally a particle may wander too close to Earth and succumb to our planet's gravity. Entering the atmosphere at speeds of up to about 45 miles (70km) per second, the particle destroys itself by burning up, through friction with air molecules. The result is a rapidly moving streak of light in the sky which we call a meteor.

Meteors that appear at any time and from any direction in the sky are sporadic meteors, and can be observed on any clear night. However, as comets travel along their orbits, they are constantly shedding particles into space. These particles eventually become spread out along the cometary orbit. At certain times of the year, the Earth passes through the orbital paths of various comets, and large numbers of particles can enter the atmosphere, whereupon meteor activity reaches a peak. During these so-called meteor showers there is a sometimes dramatic rise in the number of observed meteors.

Because the particles from a comet are travelling through space along parallel paths, each of the resulting meteors appears to come from a particular point in the sky. This point is known as the radiant. During the course of a year there are many meteor showers, each of which has its own particular radiant. These showers are given names after the area of sky in which the radiant lies. For example, the Ophiuchids radiate from a point in the constellation Ophiuchus, while the Piscis Australids emanate from the constellation Piscis Austrinus.

ABOVE: *A bright, flaring meteor photographed to the southwest of Rigel in Orion on 16 March 1975.*

METEOR OBSERVATION

Meteor observation consists of watching for and counting meteors as they appear. The minimum duration for a meteor watch should be one hour and, as you can get pretty cold lying still for this length of time (even on summer evenings), take careful note of the points given in Observing Hints.

Meteor watching is generally carried out with the naked eye. Although meteor watches can be held on any clear night, it is best to start off by observing during an active meteor shower. Lists of forthcoming meteor showers are given in astronomical magazines. At least this way you stand a good chance of actually seeing meteor activity!

When carrying out a watch, various details should be noted for each meteor seen, including whether it is from any of the particular showers under observation (note the positions in the sky of the radiants of currently active showers prior to commencing observations), times and estimated magnitudes of particularly bright meteors, start and finish times for the watch and notes of anything that may affect the success of your observations, such as strong moonlight, intermittent cloud and so on. Many of the organizations listed in the Appendices can offer advice on meteor watches.

Guide to the Moon

With a diameter of 2,172 miles (3,476km), the Moon is over a quarter of the size of the Earth. When we look at other planet and satellite systems we see that the planet is nearly always considerably larger than its attendant satellites. There is so little difference between the sizes of Earth and Moon that the system can be regarded (as can Pluto and Charon) as a double planet.

The Formation of the Moon

The Moon is thought to have formed following a collision with the Earth by an object comparable in size to Mars. According to the so-called Collision Ejection Theory, by the time this collision took place both the Earth and the impacting body had formed metallic cores surrounded by thick mantles of rock. Following impact, the smaller object broke up, its core sticking to the Earth. The Moon was formed through the collecting together of the resulting debris which was thrown into orbit around the Earth.

Examination of the lunar rocks brought back by the Apollo astronauts has convinced astronomers of this. Both the overall density of the Moon, and its chemical composition, are similar to those of the Earth's outer layers. Of all the ideas advanced to explain the origin of the Moon, this theory is the most popular and widely accepted.

Captured Rotation

The Moon's face is familiar to many of us; it has what is called a 'captured rotation', which means that its 27·3-day period of axial rotation is the same as its orbital period around the Earth. The result is that the Moon keeps the same face turned permanently towards us.

However, the Moon's orbital speed alters slightly during this period, due to its varying distance from us. At its closest point the Moon is just 222,756 miles (356,410km) away, increasing to 254,186 miles (406,697km) at its furthest.

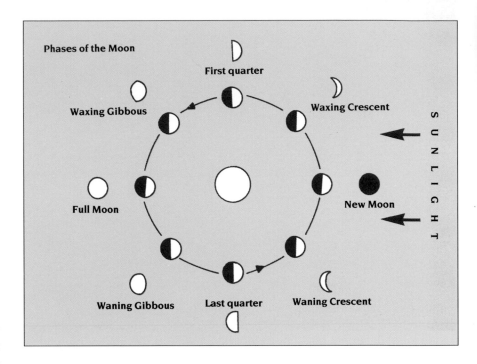

Phases of the Moon

First quarter — Waxing Gibbous — Waxing Crescent — SUNLIGHT — New Moon — Full Moon — Waning Gibbous — Last quarter — Waning Crescent

ABOVE: The orbit of the Moon as seen from outside its orbit (inner) together with its appearance at certain points in its orbit as seen from Earth.

FACING PAGE: The Moon at first and last quarter with various features identified, all of which are visible through a small telescope.

As with any orbiting body, at its furthest point (apogee) the Moon travels a little slower than when at its closest (perigee). This results in the Moon's axial rotation period and period of revolution getting slightly 'out of step' with each other, producing a kind of sideways 'wobble'. This wobble, known as libration, allows us to periodically see a short way around the lunar limb (the observable edge of the Moon). In all, we are able to observe up to 59 per cent of the lunar surface, although features lying within those areas near the limb are considerably foreshortened and consequently very difficult to see and map accurately. Examination of some of the accompanying photographs, together with a close look at the regions near the lunar limb, will show this quite well.

The Lunar Surface

Even a casual glance at the Moon will enable you to make out the two main types of lunar terrain. However, binoculars or small telescopes reveal mountain ranges, walled plains, valleys and large numbers of craters. The photographs shown here highlight notable areas of the lunar surface.

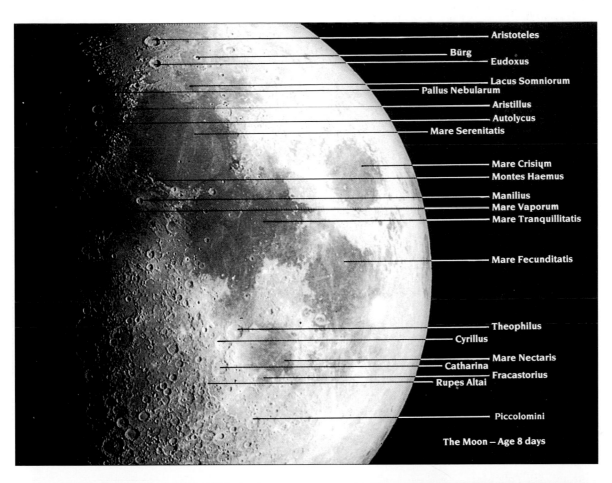

Aristoteles
Bürg
Eudoxus
Lacus Somniorum
Pallus Nebularum
Aristillus
Autolycus
Mare Serenitatis

Mare Crisium
Montes Haemus

Manilius
Mare Vaporum
Mare Tranquillitatis

Mare Fecunditatis

Theophilus
Cyrillus
Mare Nectaris
Catharina
Fracastorius
Rupes Altai

Piccolomini

The Moon – Age 8 days

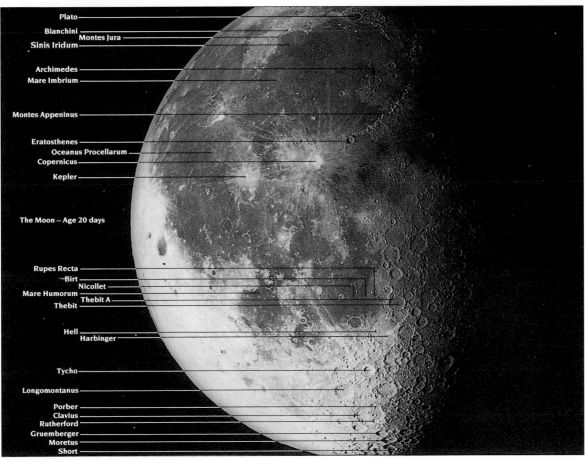

Plato
Bianchini
Montes Jura
Sinis Iridum

Archimedes
Mare Imbrium

Montes Appeninus

Eratosthenes
Oceanus Procellarum
Copernicus

Kepler

The Moon – Age 20 days

Rupes Recta
Birt
Nicollet
Mare Humorum
Thebit A
Thebit

Hell
Harbinger

Tycho

Longomontanus

Porber
Clavius
Rutherford
Gruemberger
Moretus
Short

THE MOON –
AGE FIVE DAYS

In this view of the crescent Moon (right), north is upwards. Here is shown the two main types of lunar feature, the dark lowland maria (or 'seas') contrasting with the bright, cratered uplands. Around 15 per cent of the visible lunar landscape consists of maria. Several examples can be seen here including Mare Crisium, the northernmost circular area seen near the lunar limb. To its left can be seen the vast expanse of Mare Tranquillitatis, with Mare Fecunditatis adjoining it to its immediate lower right. Mare Nectaris is the southernmost of the maria seen here, visible below Mare Tranquillitatis.

Most of the lunar surface consists of bright and heavily cratered terrain, such as that prominent on the southern half of this image. Notable examples of craters seen here include the 62 mile (100km) diameter crater Theophilus, seen on the western (left) edge of Mare Nectaris. Also prominent is Fracastorius on the southern shores of Mare Nectaris. This feature, named after the Italian astronomer Girolamo Fracastoro (1483–1553), has a diameter of 78 miles (125km). A small telescope will show that its northern wall is somewhat disintegrated, the floor of the crater extending into Mare Nectaris.

THEOPHILUS

This detailed view (facing page, top) shows the region around crater Theophilus, the prominent feature visible near the top of the picture. Its central mountain chain can be clearly seen. Just to the right (east) is the much smaller 19 mile (28km) diameter crater Madler, named after the German astronomer Johann Heinrich Madler (1794–1874). Madler lies within Mare Nectaris, part of which straddles the upper right of this view.

The crater Cyrillus can be seen just to the lower left (south west) of Theophilus, while just below this pair is the considerably disintegrated 60 mile (97km) diameter circular mountain range, Catharina.

Running across the lunar surface from a point just to the west of Catharina down towards the south east is the prominent Rupes Altai (Altai Range). This mountain chain, several hundred miles long, runs along the perimeter of Mare Nectaris. Lying at the lower end of Rupes Altai is the 58 mile (90km) diameter crater Piccolomini, whose central mountains stand out well in this view.

COPERNICUS

The prominent crater visible just to the left (west) of centre in the photograph below is Copernicus, named after the Polish astronomer Nicholaus Copernicus (1473–1543). This feature can be seen clearly through binoculars or a small telescope, standing out well against the surrounding, relatively flat landscape. Copernicus is 59 miles (93km) in diameter, and has central mountain peaks reaching a height of around 1,330yd (1200m) above the flat crater floor.

To the right (east) of Copernicus is the smaller but equally prominent crater Eratosthenes with the Montes Apenninus (Appenine Mountains) stretching away towards upper right of the picture. The Apennine Mountains lie across the south-eastern borders of Mare Imbrium (Sea of Rains), part of which can be seen running across the top of the picture.

The flooded crater Archimedes can be discerned towards the top of the picture, above the north eastern reaches of the Apennine Mountains.

PLATO AND SINUS IRIDUM

The bright, 60 mile (100km) diameter walled plain Plato can be seen at left, almost at the centre of the picture, with Sinus Iridum (Bay of Rainbows) prominent to the lower left (south-west), lying on the shores of Mare Imbrium. Sinus Iridum is bordered by Montes Jura (Jura Mountains), the bright 25 mile (40km) diameter crater Bianchini visible part way along the range. The dark reaches of Mare Imbrium occupy most of the southern half of this image.

The dark lunar plains were formed between three and four billion years ago as the result of lava flows from the lunar interior which filled the low lying areas of the lunar surface. Prior to the invention of the telescope, it was widely believed that features like Mare Imbrium were actually expanses of water, although we now know that there is no water on the lunar surface. However, the original names given to these areas, such as Mare Serenitatis (Sea of Serenity), Palus Nebularum (Marsh of Mists) and Oceanus Procellarum (Ocean of Storms) are still used.

PLATO AND ARCHIMEDES

By the time the lunar maria had been formed, the main period of meteoritic bombardment that had peppered the surface of the Moon and other rocky planets had subsided. The comparative lack of cratering on the maria indicates that these areas were formed relatively recently after the main period of meteoritic bombardment.

The relative absence of cratering in the lunar maria is illustrated well on the facing page (left) of Mare Imbrium (lower left) and Mare Serenitatis to its right (east). The crater Plato can be seen on the northern shores of Mare Imbrium. The trio of craters prominent just below the centre of the picture are Archimedes (the largest) together with the pair Aristillus (upper) and Autolycus to the right (east) of Archimedes. Small telescopes will bring out the three peaks on the floor of Aristillus.

The lower border of this view is occupied by the northern shores of Mare Vaporum (Sea of Vapours), with the bright crater Manilius seen at lower right of picture. Just above Manilius and jutting out from the eastern edge of the picture, is the Montes Haemus (Haemus Mountains) range forming a joint border between Mare Vaporum and Mare Serenitatis.

CLAVIUS

The prominent feature at the centre of the picture shown below is the famous 140 mile (225km) diameter walled plain Clavius. This region is located in the area adjacent to the lunar south pole and contains many craters. The two craters situated on the walls of Clavius are Porter (top) and Rutherford, while below (south) is the trio of craters Gruemberger, Moretus and Short. To the upper left (north-west) of Clavius is the crater Longomontanus. Situated near the terminator (ie the boundary between the sunlit and dark areas of a planet – or, in this case, the Moon), the floor of Longomontanus is in deep shadow, sunrise yet to take place.

GIBBOUS MOON WITH TYCHO

This view (right) of a gibbous Moon shows Tycho and its prominent ray system in the lunar southern hemisphere. Tycho is typical of several other young lunar craters in that it has an associated system of rays. In some cases, these rays can stretch up to 625 miles (1,000km). They are difficult or impossible to see under low illumination, and are best seen when the Moon is at or near full phase. Their appearance suggests that these systems originated as the result of material being ejected following the impacts that formed their associated craters. A similar ray system can be seen emerging from the crater Copernicus, located just above the lunar equator to the upper left of Tycho.

THE STRAIGHT WALL

To the upper left (north-west) of the above image can be seen part of Mare Nubium (Sea of Clouds) containing the three small but prominent craters Nicollet (upper left), Birt and Thebit A, the latter located on the rim of its larger companion Thebit. Just to the right (east) of Birt, and running roughly from north to south, is Rupes Recta (the Straight Wall). This feature is one of the most unusual on the Moon and is best seen when illuminated from the east when it can cast a wide shadow across the surrounding flat terrain. At these times it is often visible through binoculars, and clearly visible through small telescopes. Just below Mare Nubium is the disintegrated walled plain Horbinger with the small, 21 mile (33km) diameter crater Hell on its western flanks. This feature is named after Maximilian Hell (1720–1792), the Hungarian astronomer who founded the Vienna Observatory.

Eclipses

Although the Sun is considerably larger than the Moon, it is also much further away. Its distance is such that both the Sun and Moon have similar apparent diameters. This leads to one of nature's most awesome spectacles which occurs when the Moon passes in front of the Sun, temporarily hiding our parent star from view.

SOLAR ECLIPSES

Total solar eclipses occur if the Sun, Moon and Earth are exactly aligned and the Sun is completely hidden, and a partial eclipse if only part of the Sun is obscured. Annular eclipses occur during an exact alignment if the Moon is at its furthest point from us. Its apparent diameter will be less, and the Sun will be seen as a ring around the Moon. The term 'annular' is derived from the Latin word *annulus* meaning 'ring'.

The total solar eclipse of 11 June 1983 as seen from Java is shown in the photograph at right. During this and other total solar eclipses, the Sun's outer atmosphere, or corona, can be seen surrounding the lunar disc. The corona is visible to the unaided eye only during total solar eclipses, the glare of the Sun normally swamping its relatively feeble glow.

LUNAR ECLIPSES

Because the Moon's orbital plane is tilted with respect to the plane of the Earth's orbit around the Sun, it normally passes either above or below the Earth's shadow. Lunar eclipses take place at full Moon when our satellite is opposite the Sun in the sky. For a total lunar eclipse to occur, the three bodies must be exactly aligned. This can only happen if the Moon is at the point in its orbit where its orbital path takes it across the plane of the Earth's orbit.

Total lunar eclipses occur if the entire lunar disc passes through the dark, central umbra of the Earth's shadow, a partial eclipse taking place when only part of the Moon enters this region. During a lunar eclipse, the curved shadow of the Earth can be seen crossing the lunar disc.

The area of partial shadow surrounding the umbra is called the penumbra. If the Moon only passes through this region a penumbral eclipse occurs these are very hard to detect as the darkening effect of the Earth's penumbral shadow is very slight.

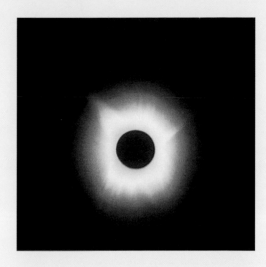

When the Moon passes into the Earth's shadow, the sunlight which normally illuminates the lunar surface is cut off and our satellite is plunged into darkness. However, it is only very rarely that the Moon disappears completely from view. A small amount of sunlight is usually bent onto the lunar surface by the Earth's atmosphere, resulting in the Moon taking on a deep coppery-red colour. This colouration is evident in the view of the total lunar eclipse of 9 January 1982, shown below.

The Starry Sky

On clear, dark, moonless nights, the sky seems to teem with millions of stars, although in reality you can never see more than a couple of thousand at any one time when looking with the unaided eye. Every star that you see belongs to a particular grouping, or constellation, of stars. However, the constellations which we see in the sky and which grace the pages of star atlases are nothing more than chance alignments. The stars that make up the star patterns we see, actually lie at vastly differing distances from us, and only appear close to each other because they lie in more or less the same direction as seen from Earth.

Many constellations are named after mythological characters, and were given their names thousands of years ago. However, those lying close to the south celestial pole were discovered only during the last century or so, resulting in many of them having modern-sounding names such as Octans (the Octant) and Microscopium (the Microscope).

Over the centuries, many different suggestions for new constellations have been put forward by astronomers who, for one reason or another, felt the need to add new groupings to star charts. Many of these astronomers drew up their own charts of the sky, incorporating their new groups onto them. Prominent here was Johann Bode who, towards the end of the eighteenth century, created a number of new constellations, many with cumbersome names, including Sceptrum Brandenburgicum (The Sceptre of Brandenburg), Felis (the Cat) and Quadrans Muralis (the Mural Quadrant). Although these have since been rejected, the latter has been immortalized by the annual Quadrantid meteor shower, the radiant of which lies in an area of sky formerly occupied by Quadrans Muralis. Earlier this century the International Astronomical Union systemized matters by adopting an official list of 88 accepted constellations.

Measuring Stellar Distances

In order to express large distances in space, astronomers use a unit of length known as a *light-year*, rather than miles or kilometres. To describe the distances to remote stars in miles would be like expressing the distance across North America in inches, so large and unwieldy would be the numbers! A light-year is equal to the distance that a ray of light, travelling at 186,000 miles (300,000km) per second, would traverse in a year. This is equal to 5,910,000,000,000 miles (9,460,000,000,000km)! In other words, to say the star Vega in Lyra is 27 light-years away means that the light we are seeing from the star today set off towards us 27 years ago.

In 1838, the German astronomer Friedrich Bessell carried out a series of observations of the star 61 Cygni, which, he calculated, was 10.3 light-years from Earth. Bessell's observations used the idea of trigonometrical parallax, whereby if a nearby object is viewed from two different locations, it will appear to shift slightly when seen against a more distant background.

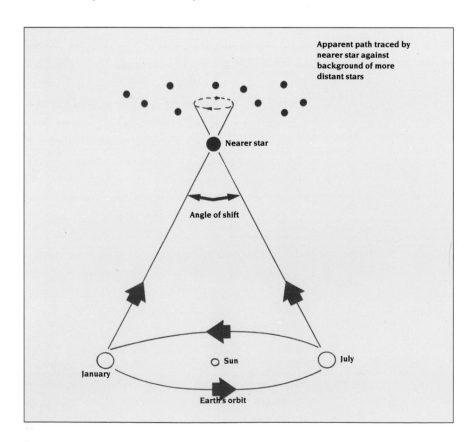

Apparent path traced by nearer star against background of more distant stars

Nearer star

Angle of shift

January

Sun

July

Earth's orbit

ANGULAR MEASUREMENT

Distances between points on the celestial sphere are expressed in angles, as are the sizes of objects such as the Sun, Moon and planets. The largest angles, such as the distances across constellations or between individual stars, are measured in degrees, while smaller angles are expressed in minutes (denoted ') and seconds (denoted "). One degree is split up into 60 minutes and each minute into 60 seconds. A distance expressed this way indicates the angle that would be formed at the eye by two lines of sight, one from each of the two points on the celestial sphere.

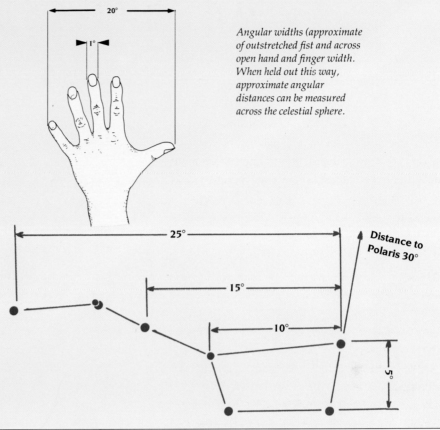

Angular widths (approximate of outstretched fist and across open hand and finger width. When held out this way, approximate angular distances can be measured across the celestial sphere.

The principle of parallax can be illustrated by a simple experiment where you hold your finger at arm's length, lined up with a distant object such as a tree. View it alternately with your left and right eyes. The result of viewing your finger from slightly different directions will be to make it appear to shift in relation to the tree. Knowing both the angle by which your finger appeared to shift (the angle of parallax) and the distance between your eyes enables the distance to your finger to be calculated using simple trigonometry (see feature above).

What Bessell did was to determine the angle by which 61 Cygni appeared to shift against the background of more distant stars when viewed from opposite ends of the Earth's orbit around the Sun. He knew the diameter of the Earth's orbit, and was therefore able to use trigonometry to work out the distance to the star. This principle of determining stellar distances had long been known, yet it took several attempts by different astronomers before it was used successfully by Bessell. Bessell's skills as an observer, coupled with his access to telescopes and equipment, which were more powerful than those of his predecessors, enabled Bessell to measure 61 Cygni's tiny parallax shift.

This method can only be used for relatively close stars. The further away a star is, the smaller (and more difficult to measure) will be its angular shift against the stellar background. Similarly, the further away your finger is from your eyes, the smaller is its angular shift against the background when viewed through each eye alternately. Beyond 70 light-years or so (within which radius there are around 1,400 stars) its distance must be calculated differently. In these cases astronomers compare a star of known distance and one of the same type but lying at an unknown distance from us. Assuming that two stars of similar type will have similar luminosities, astronomers can work the distance to the more distant star by comparing both its apparent and actual brightnesses. The accuracy of this method hinges on astronomers being able to accurately access a distant star's type and brightness.

Light-years are not the only unit of distance used by astronomers. Another unit is the *parsec*, equal to 3·26 light-years. This is the distance at which a star would subtend an angle of PARallax equal to one SECond of arc. In reality, there are no stars as close as this, the nearest (apart from the Sun) being Proxima Centauri, which lies at a distance of 4·3 light-years (1·32 parsecs).

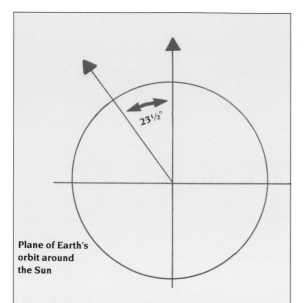

Plane of Earth's orbit around the Sun

Tilt of the Earth's axis

THE SEASONS

The tilt of the Earth's axis relative to the plane of its orbit around the Sun gives rise to the seasons. In June the northern hemisphere is tilted towards the Sun and from locations in the northern hemisphere the Sun will appear to be higher in the sky. This produces longer, warmer days in what will be summer in the northern hemisphere. Because the southern hemisphere is tilted away from the Sun at this time, the Sun will appear to be lower in the sky, days will be shorter and cooler and southern winter will take place. The situation is reversed six months later. In December, the northern hemisphere is tilted away from the Sun and the southern hemisphere towards it, giving northern winter and southern summer.

The Brightness of Stars

The system of classifying stars according to their brightness, or magnitude, devised by the Greek astronomer Hipparchus in around 150 BC, is still in use today. Hipparchus graded stars into six classes, the brightest being graded as first class and the faintest as sixth class.

However, because Hipparchus' estimates were made through naked eye observation only, his grading was approximate at best. Today's astronomers can now estimate magnitudes to within a margin of 0·01, although the same basic system is used. Unlike Hipparchus we now use negative values. The brighter the object, the lower its magnitude number, with minus values being used for the brightest objects. Sirius, the brightest star in the sky, has a magnitude of −1·42.

In 1856 Norman Pogson established a more accurate definition of stellar magnitude by stating that a star of magnitude 1 was 100 times as bright as one of magnitude 6. Taking this a step further, we define a star of magnitude 3 as being 2·512 ($^5\sqrt{100}$) times as bright as one of magnitude 4, 6·31 (2·512 × 2·512) times as bright as a star of magnitude 5 and so on.

Binoculars will show objects down to around magnitude 9, whilst a small telescope will reveal stars of magnitude 10 under good viewing conditions. The world's largest instruments bring out objects of around magnitude 26 or even fainter.

The brightness of all celestial objects are expressed with the magnitude scale. The brightest object of all, the Sun, has a magnitude of −26·8 whilst that of the full Moon is around −12·7. The magnitude of Pluto hovers at around −14, considerably fainter than brilliant Venus, the brightest of the planets with a maximum magnitude of −4·4.

Absolute Magnitudes

The above system expresses the apparent brightnesses of stars and other celestial objects, although it offers no real guide as to their true luminosities. This is achieved by using the system of absolute magnitude, which defines the magnitude a star would have if placed at a distance of 10 parsecs or 32·6 light-years.

The star Rigel, in Orion, has an apparent magnitude of 0·14 and lies at a distance of 900 light-years. Alpha Centauri appears brighter at magnitude −0·27, although its distance is just 4·34 light-years. Rigel is actually many times more luminous than Alpha Centauri, and only appears fainter because it lies so much further away. If both of these stars were placed at a distance of 10 parsecs, the visual magnitude of Alpha Centauri would be +4·4 whilst that of Rigel would be −7·1!

Day and Night

A 'day' is the word generally used to describe the time it takes for the Earth to rotate on its axis. The rotation of the Earth causes night and day. Daytime occurs for the side of the Earth facing the Sun, night taking place when that side is facing away. The rotation of the Earth also causes the stars and other objects in the sky to appear to rise and set, this apparent motion always being from east to west across the sky.

SOLAR AND SIDEREAL DAYS

The true rotational period of the Earth is 23 hours 56 minutes 4·09 seconds. This period is called a sidereal day (from the Latin *sidus* meaning 'star'), and is equal to the period between successive passages across the meridian of a star. (The meridian is an imaginary line reaching from the north point on the horizon, through the celestial pole and overhead point and down to the south point on the horizon. It is not fixed but refers to the sky that an observer sees from any-where on the Earth's surface.) When a star crosses the meridian it is at its greatest angular distance (or alti-tude – *see* pages 32 and 33) from the horizon. At this point it is said to 'culminate'. If a star is on the meri-dian at midnight on a particular night, it will reach the same position just under four minutes sooner the following night.

A solar day is 24 hours long, and is the interval between successive meridian passages (noons) of the Sun. However, the solar day is a little longer than the sidereal day. This is a direct result of the Earth orbiting the Sun. As it does so, we see the Sun from a slightly different position from day to day. As the Earth advances along its orbit, the Sun seems to shift slowly eastwards. This can be pictured better by imagining you are walking in an anti-clockwise direction (corres-ponding to the direction of travel of the Earth in its orbit) around a model of the Sun in the centre of a room. As you travel in your 'orbit', the model Sun will *appear* to travel from right to left (corresponding in an eastwardly shift of the Sun in the sky) against the walls of the room. This effect is caused by *your* motion, the solar model remaining stationary. Because the Sun shifts slightly eastwards from day to day, it rises a little later each morning. It is because the Sun has to 'catch up' in this way that the solar day is slightly longer than the sidereal day. The Sun therefore appears to travel completely round the sky during the course of a year.

The Zodiac

The apparent motion of the Sun through the sky means that we see it superimposed against a different point on the celestial sphere from day to day. Its apparent course around the sky appears to take it from west to east through a band of constellations. We call this band the Zodiac, with the actual path of the Sun through the Zodiac being called the Ecliptic.

The constellations that form the Zodiac are Pisces, Aries, Taurus, Gemini, Cancer, Leo, Virgo, Libra, Scorpius, Sagittarius, Capricornus and Aquarius. It is not only the Sun which appears to travel through the Zodiac: because the planets orbit the Sun in more or less the same plane as each other, they too are always seen against the backdrop of zodiacal constellations.

The Celestial Sphere

The celestial sphere is the imaginary sphere of sky that completely surrounds the Earth. For simplicity, the stars are considered to be fixed on the celestial sphere, whilst the apparent motion of the Sun and the actual orbits of the planets result in their appear-ing to travel around the celestial sphere against the backdrop of stars.

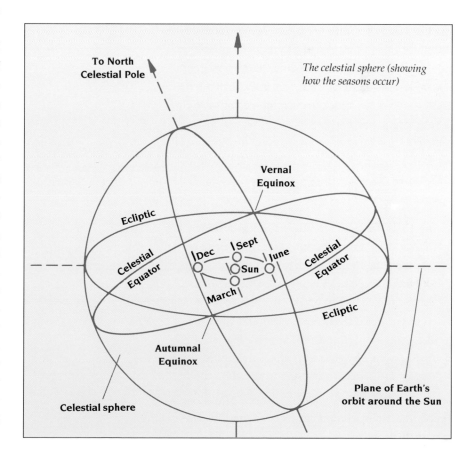

The celestial sphere (showing how the seasons occur)

To North Celestial Pole

Vernal Equinox

Ecliptic

Celestial Equator

Dec | Sept | June
Sun
March

Celestial Equator

Ecliptic

Autumnal Equinox

Celestial sphere

Plane of Earth's orbit around the Sun

As well as giving rise to night and day, the rotation of the Earth on its axis causes the apparent rotation of the celestial sphere around the Earth. This rotation is centred on an imaginary axis passing through the Earth and joining the north and south celestial poles. These are points on the celestial sphere lying directly above the north and south terrestrial poles, through which projections of the Earth's axis would intercept the celestial sphere.

The north celestial pole (NCP) is marked by the star Polaris in Ursa Minor, while the nearest star to the south celestial pole (SCP) is the faint Sigma Octantis. As the Earth rotates, the stars on the celestial sphere appear to revolve around these two stars.

Just as the celestial poles are projections of the Earth's axis of rotation, the celestial equator is a projection of the Earth's equator onto the sky. Just as its terrestrial counterpart is located at 90° from each pole, the celestial equator lies at an angular distance of 90° from each of the celestial poles.

Solstices

The point at which the Sun is at its maximum angular distance northwards of the celestial equator is called the summer solstice, and in the Earth's northern hemisphere this occurs on or around 21 June when that hemisphere is tilted towards the Sun. Similarly, winter solstice occurs on or around 22 December in the northern hemisphere when the Earth's southern hemisphere is tilted towards the Sun. At this time, the Sun attains its highest point in the sky for southern hemisphere observers.

THE ECLIPTIC

As well as creating the seasons, the tilt of the Earth's axis affects the apparent motion of the Sun through the sky. In northern summer, the Sun appears to be higher in the sky than in northern winter. In other words, during the course of a year, the Sun appears to travel not only from west to east (due to the motion of the Earth around the Sun) through the sky, but also alternately northwards and southwards (due to the alternate tilt towards and away from the Sun of the Earth's axis).

The Earth is tilted at 23½° relative to the plane of its orbit around the Sun. Therefore, when the northern hemisphere is tilted directly towards the Sun in June, the Sun will be 23½° above the celestial equator. At this time, from latitude 23½°N (the Tropic of Cancer) the Sun will be directly overhead at noon and the northern hemisphere experiences its longest day and shortest night. On 22 December each year, when the southern hemisphere is tilted towards the Sun, the Sun will be overhead from latitude 23½°S (the Tropic of Capricorn).

The solstices (the points at which the Sun reaches its highest and lowest positions in the sky) correspond to the 'crests' of the apparent wave-like journey of the Sun through the sky.

EQUINOXES

As the Sun appears to travel northwards in its journey around the Zodiac, it crosses the celestial equator at a point known as the vernal, or spring, equinox. Similarly, as it moves southwards it crosses the celestial equator at a point called the autumnal equinox. When the Sun is located at either of the equinoxes, day and night are the same length.

Altitude of the Poles

The altitude of a star or other celestial object is its angular distance above the horizon. The altitude of the NCP (north celestial pole) above the northern horizon (or the SCP above the southern horizon) is equal to the latitude of the observer. An observer at the north pole (latitude 90°N), would see the NCP directly overhead, at an altitude of 90°. In other words, it would be at the zenith. This is not a fixed point, but refers to the point in the sky above the observer.

The further away you come from the north pole, the lower the NCP will be in the sky. From Paris (latitude 49°N) it will have an altitude of 49°, and from the equator (latitude 0°), it will have an altitude of 0°. From the equator Polaris will be seen on the northern horizon and from south of the equator it will be hidden by the body of the Earth and will not be seen at all.

The same is true for Sigma Octantis, the star marking the SCP, as viewed from the southern hemisphere. From the equator it will be seen at around the level of the southern horizon, while from the south pole it will be visible at the zenith. From Melbourne (latitude 38°S) it will be 38° above the southern horizon. The celestial poles lie at compass points north and

south. In other words, you would be looking due north if you were gazing at Polaris and due south if gazing at Sigma Octantis.

It is not only Polaris that would be hidden from view to an observer south of the equator. Stars near the NCP would also be hidden, more and more stars being lost to view the further south you go. The same is true for observers north of the equator. The further north you travel, the more stars disappear below the southern horizon. Consequently, from any latitude north (or south) of the equator, there are stars permanently hidden around the SCP (or NCP). From observing locations actually at the north (or south) poles, only those stars north (or south) of the celestial equator will ever be seen. For example, the well-known group of stars we call the Plough lie so close to the NCP that they are never seen by observers in the Falkland Islands, in much the same way that the southern constellation Crux is permanently hidden to observers in Great Britain.

ABOVE: Venus (bottom) together with open star clusters Hyades and Pleiades in the Sunset sky, photographed in April 1978.

CIRCUMPOLAR STARS

If the angular distance of a star from the celestial pole is less than the latitude of the observer, that star will never set as seen from that latitude, and will remain permanently above the horizon. Such stars are referred to as circumpolar stars. In other words, for an observer in Istanbul (latitude 41°N), all stars within 41° of the NCP will trace out circles centred on the NCP and will never touch the horizon. Dubhe (Alpha Ursae Majoris), which is 30° from the NCP, will be circumpolar, while Castor (Alpha Geminorum), located 58° from the NCP, will not. The same applies to both the northern and southern hemispheres. For an observer on the equator (latitude 0°), there will be no circumpolar stars, while from the poles, all stars will be circumpolar.

Another way to determine whether a star is circumpolar is to subtract your latitude from 90°. In the case of Istanbul, this would give a value of $(90-41) = 49°$ All stars north of declination $+49°$ (see below) will be circumpolar. Similarly, an observer in Istanbul will never see stars south of declination −49°, as they will never rise above the southern horizon. The same principle works (albeit in reverse) for southern hemisphere observers.

Precession of the Equinoxes

Just as the celestial poles trace out circles in the northern and southern skies, the celestial equator also travels the ecliptic. The two points at which the celestial equator crosses the ecliptic are known as the equinoxes. These travel along the ecliptic, taking 25,800 years to complete one journey around the sky. The position of the vernal equinox (also known as the First Point of Aries) is constantly changing. Around 2,000 years ago it lay in the constellation of Aries (hence its popular name), although it should now be known as the First Point of Pisces as it has since moved into this constellation. A few centuries from now it will enter Aquarius.

Right Ascension and Declination

Although the system is not used in the finder charts in this book, astronomers usually express the locations of stars and other celestial objects on the celestial sphere in terms of right ascension and declination. Generally speaking, these coordinates are the celestial equivalent of longitude and latitude on the Earth's surface, although there are important differences.

Declination is simply the angular distance of an object above or below the celestial equator. Polaris, located almost at the NCP, has a declination of +89° 15′ 51″ (the + denoting a declination north of the

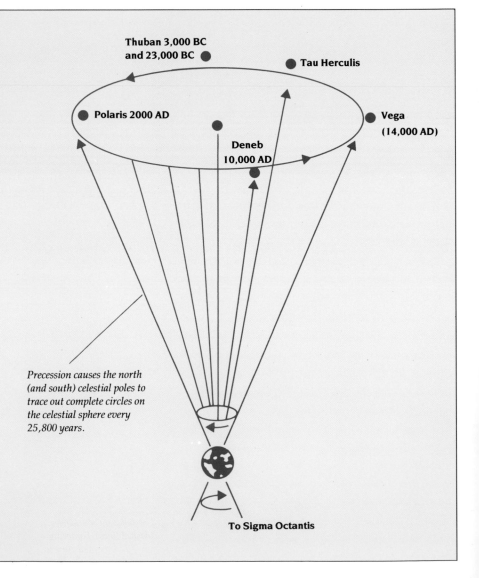

PRECESSION

The position of the celestial poles are slowly changing. This is because of a 'wobble' in the Earth's axis of rotation. This wobble, which is similar to that of a spinning top which is slowing down, is called precession and is caused by the gravitational influences of the Sun and Moon on the Earth's equatorial bulge. Each wobble takes 25,800 years, during which time the celestial poles trace out circles on the celestial sphere.

The change in position of the north celestial pole (NCP) in relation to the stars is shown here. The SCP traces out a similar circle amongst the stars in the region of the SCP. The radii of the circles traced out by the celestial poles are 23·50°, which is the angular tilt of the Earth's axis relative to the plane of its orbit around the Sun.

At the current time Polaris lies very close to the NCP, although this has not always been the case. Because of precession, the star Thuban in the constellation Draco marked the position of the NCP around 4,500 years ago. Eventually, some 12,000 years from now, the brilliant star Vega in Lyra will mark this position.

Precession causes the north (and south) celestial poles to trace out complete circles on the celestial sphere every 25,800 years.

Thuban 3,000 BC and 23,000 BC

Tau Herculis

Polaris 2000 AD

Deneb 10,000 AD

Vega (14,000 AD)

To Sigma Octantis

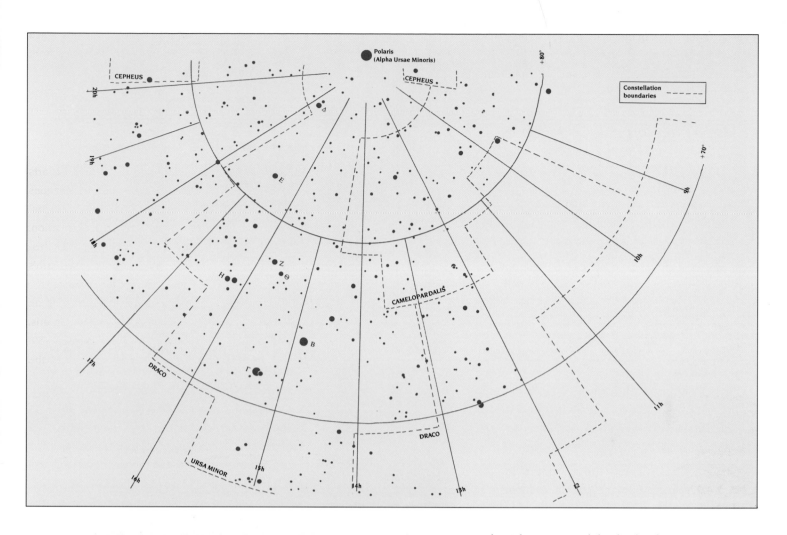

ABOVE: *The Milky Way in Scorpius with part of Sagittarius visible in the left hand section.*

TOP: *A chart of Ursa Minor showing Right Ascension and Declination (solid lines), constellation boundaries (dashed lines), bordering constellations and stars to around 8th magnitude.*

celestial equator), while the bright star Canopus in Carina has a declination of −52° 58′ 32″ (the − denoting a declination south of the celestial equator). The declination of the Sun at the vernal or autumnal equinox is 0°.

Right ascension is a little more complicated and is measured eastwards from the vernal equinox. Expressed in hours, minutes and seconds of time (as opposed to degrees, minutes and seconds of angle), the right ascension of a star is the interval between the culmination of the vernal equinox and the culmination of the star. In other words, the right ascension of Rigel in Orion is 05h 14m 32·2s, which means that it crosses the meridian 5 hours, 14 minutes and 32·2 seconds after the vernal equinox.

As we have seen, the precession of the equinoxes described above causes the vernal equinox to travel around the ecliptic. This results in slight changes in the right ascensions and declinations of stars. Because of this, stellar coordinates need to be periodically revised. The positions used here and in the Appendices are those valid in AD 2000, and will be sufficiently accurate until several years into the next century.

Observing Hints

Get at Home Amongst the Stars

Identification of the constellations visible from your latitude is not a difficult prospect, and will help you to feel at home under the sky. Some constellations are prominent and easily picked out. Identification of these groups, the ranks of which include Cassiopeia, Ursa Major, Orion, Canis Major, Crux and Centaurus, should be the main priority. These can then be followed up by picking out some of the more obscure constellations by using the above groups as guides.

A number of constellations can be used to lead the way to other groups. A famous example is Ursa Minor, its brightest star Polaris found by extending the line from Merak through Dubhe, the two stars forming the end of the 'bowl' in the Plough (*see* North Circumpolar Stars on page 42). There are many other similar 'signposts' in the sky and eventually, with enthusiasm and a little patience, you will learn your way around the night sky.

DARK ADAPTATION

Prior to carrying out any form of observation, it is important to get your eyes dark adapted. Normally, under well-lit conditions, the eye pupils are almost closed, although in the dark, they open up to their maximum extent to allow as much light as possible into the eye. This helps you see more clearly under dim conditions and facilitates the location of faint objects. You should allow at least 15 minutes for your eyes to become dark adapted, although full dark adaptation may take anything up to 45 minutes. Any illumination used for reading star charts and so on while observing should be in the form of a red light, as the human eye is hardly sensitive to light of this colour. A flashlight with a red filter will not ruin your dark adaptation.

AVERTED VISION

'Averted vision' is a very useful technique for observing faint objects. This involves looking slightly to one side of the object under observation. By doing so you allow the light emitted by the object to fall on a more sensitive part of the retina. Although you are not looking directly at the object, it is surprising how much more detail comes into view. This technique is also useful when observing double stars which have components of greatly contrasting brightnesses. Often, although direct vision may not reveal the glow of a faint companion star in the glare of a much brighter primary, averted vision may well bring the fainter star into view.

SOMETHING IN THE AIR!

Turbulence in the atmosphere, measurement of which is referred to as 'seeing' by astronomers, can impair observation by making telescopic images seem to flicker. Higher magnifications tend to emphasize the distortion produced on nights of 'bad seeing', so lower powers are often preferred at these times. Observing over houses or other heated buildings will also affect the telescopic image, the warmth emitted by the dwelling causing atmospheric turbulence above it.

The atmosphere impairs observations in another way. The more atmosphere that the light from a star or other deep sky object has to pass through, the more its light is absorbed and the fainter it appears. Close to the Earth's surface are found substances such as water vapour and dust, which hinder observation. High altitude observing sites (the type of site preferred for the world's major observatories) take you above much of this pollution and provide darker and clearer skies.

LIGHT POLLUTION

Artificial lighting is another problem. Much of the glow from streetlights, advertisement signs and other types of man-made illumination tends to find its way up into the atmosphere, becoming scattered by the dust and other pollutants mentioned above. This produces a glow of light above cities and towns. This so-called light pollution artificially brightens the night sky and renders many faint deep sky objects invisible. Taking yourself even a few miles out into the surrounding countryside may reduce the effects of this considerably.

Looking into Deep Space

Many deep sky objects, such as open clusters, galaxies or nebulae, have large apparent diameters. Wide fields of view are required in order that they are seen to their full effect. Globular clusters are much more compact, and generally appear as faint, diffuse, star-like objects. Their compactness means that higher magnifications may often be used to good effect. Some globulars are quite compact and only their out-lying stars are visible in amateur telescopes. Others, like Omega Centauri, are much more loosely structured, and even small telescopes can resolve large numbers of stars in these systems.

Nebulae and galaxies often provide very little contrast against the background sky and can be difficult to see. Under 'normal' urban skies, many galaxies and nebulae are practically invisible. Low power eyepieces are essential, and a sky that is clear and moonless is highly preferable. Deep sky observation should really be avoided when the Moon is at or near full

phase, as strong moonlight can considerably brighten the background sky. When searching for galaxies or nebulae, identify the area of sky containing the object, then 'sweep' the telescope back and forth across it. The sometimes minimal difference in contrast between the nebula or galaxy and the background sky may then be increased.

STAR HOPPING

Although objects can be located by using their celestial coordinates (*see* The Starry Sky) and telescopes equipped with setting circles (*see* Looking at the Sky), the method used in the charts in this book for deep sky object location is 'star hopping'. This is one of the best methods for locating deep sky objects and is simple both in principle and operation. First of all, a reasonably bright star lying in the same area of sky as the object you are seeking is identified. Then, using binoculars (or your telescope finder) you can bring the object into the field of view by 'hopping' from one star to another, using patterns or lines of stars. Locating objects in this way allows you to build up a working knowledge of star patterns within the regions of sky occupied by different objects and, after several observations, it becomes much easier to pick out the object again purely by memory and without the use of the start charts.

A B O V E L E F T : *Casual sweeping of the night sky through binoculars or a small telescope may occasionally reveal objects like the appropriately-named Coathanger Cluster. This is a cluster of around 40 stars lying at a distance of 400 light years.*

B E L O W : *The globular cluster 47 Tucanae is widely regarded as being one of the finest objects of its type in the sky.*

GET PROPERLY DRESSED!

It is surprising just how cold you can get when observing the night sky, even during summer months. After all, you may be sitting or lying motionless for most of the time. When carrying out naked-eye observation, sleeping bags, sun loungers (or deckchairs) are a good combination, providing warmth and a comfortable observing position. Anoraks also provide warmth, as well as plenty of pocket space for eyepieces and so on. Warm garments should be worn under this, and thick trousers and socks and comfortably-fitting boots or shoes. Also, because most body heat is lost through the head, some form of headgear is essential. Gloves of the 'fingerless' type will provide protection for the hands while at the same time allowing for easier handling of eyepieces and other equipment.

Variable Stars

Not all stars have constant luminosities. Variable stars fluctuate in brightness over relatively short periods. These changes are caused by either the intervention of another star or gas and dust (extrinsic variables), or by changes or pulsations occurring within the stars themselves (intrinsic variables). These two categories are further divided into different individual types.

Whatever the type of variable, the changes which occur in its light output are represented by a graph or *light curve*, which plots the observed variations in magnitude against time. The point at which the star is at its faintest is called the *minimum*. Similarly the point of greatest brilliance is classed as the *maximum*. The difference between minimum and maximum is referred to as the *amplitude*, while the time taken for a complete cycle of variations is known as the *period*.

Extrinsic Variables

The classic extrinsic variables are the eclipsing binaries, systems of two stars orbiting their common centre of gravity. As seen from Earth, the two stars alternately hide all or part of each other from view, resulting in variations in their overall light output.

One of the most interesting variable stars, and indeed the most famous of the eclipsing binaries is Algol, or Beta Persei. The variations of Algol have been observed for centuries, although it was the English astronomer John Goodricke who, in 1782, suggested that Algol was a binary star with one component very much darker than the other. Because the orbital plane of the two stars in the Algol system lies in our line of sight, each star periodically passes in front of its companion, thereby causing an eclipse. The eclipse is particularly pronounced every 2.87 days when the brighter component is temporarily obscured by the darker star.

Another type of extrinsic variable are the T Tauri stars, young stars enveloped in wreaths of gas and dust ejected during their settling down to a stable period of evolution. Their variations are totally unpredictable, and are caused by the interspersion of this material.

Intrinsic Variables

Intrinsic variables change in brightness because of pulsations or eruptions taking place within the star itself. The supergiant variable stars known as Cepheids are the most famous class of intrinsic variable. These highly luminous objects, named after Delta Cephei (the first star of its type to be discovered), have short periods of 1–55 days, and variations in their light outputs of no more than 1.5 magnitudes. Cepheid light curves are all similar, the usually irregular drop to minimum always being slower than the subsequent smooth rise to maximum. Delta Cephei itself varies between magnitudes 3.6 and 4.3 over a well-determined period of 5.36634 days.

THE PERIOD-LUMINOSITY RELATIONSHIP

Because of their high luminosities, Cepheids can be seen over tremendous distances. In fact, it was through the observation of Cepheids in the Small Magellanic Cloud (now known to lie at a distance of around 200,000 light-years) that the American astronomer Henrietta Swan Leavitt was able to announce a link between the actual luminosities and periods of Cepheids. Leavitt assumed, correctly, that all the Cepheids under observation were at roughly the same distance. She

BELOW: *Light curve of Algol (Beta Persei) with magnitude plotted at left and time along the bottom axis. The pronounced drop to minimum magnitude takes place very 2.87 days (plotted as 68.9 hours on this diagram).*

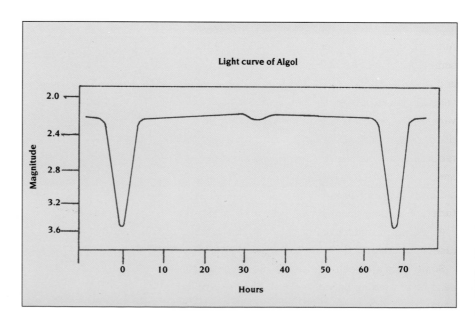

noticed that Cepheids with shorter periods were always fainter than those whose periods of variability were longer, arriving at the conclusion that Cepheids with longer periods had greater actual luminosities and were more powerful.

Leavitt's pioneering work in determining the Cepheid Period-Luminosity Relationship allowed astronomers to calculate the distances to Cepheids. The longer the period of a Cepheid, the brighter the star.

Once the actual brightness was calculated and compared to the apparent brightness, the distance to the Cepheid could be worked out. Distances to external galaxies in which Cepheids were observed could now be calculated; indeed, it was after the observation of Cepheids in nearby galaxies by Edwin Hubble in the 1920s that he was able to show that these huge stellar gatherings were systems well outside our own.

Long Period Variables

The most famous long period variable is Mira, or Omicron Ceti. Mira was the first variable star to be discovered and is typical of long period variables, in that its maxima and minima are not constant. Long period variables are the most abundant type of variable, and around 4,000 are known. Their period can be anything from 200 to 400 days and all vary considerably in brightness but with no definite regularity.

Other Types of Variable

Amongst the many other types of variable are the semi-regular variables, whose variations are only slight and whose periods are very difficult to detect. Irregular variables have no regular periods at all. R Coronae variables, named after the first star of its type to be discovered, undergo sudden and unpredictable reductions in brightness. For most of the time they are seen to pulsate slightly at maximum brightness, although they can suddenly drop by up to 9 magnitudes, remaining at minimum for up to a year.

R Coronae variables are well worth monitoring in case they suddenly decrease in brightness.

Some stars are seen to increase rapidly in brightness before fading back to normal. These so-called novae are fairly common and there have been many

ABOVE: *The top photograph shows Nova Vulpeculae at magnitude 6.5 in late October 1976. The nova appeared next to the Coathanger Cluster, seen here near centre of picture. The bottom picture shows the nova at 8th magnitude in early November 1976.*

spectacular examples observed. Recurrent novae are seen to brighten on more than one occasion, although their increases are nowhere near as large or dramatic as the novae. Dwarf novae are similar, although their increases occur at a much more frequent rate.

All novae are members of close binary systems in which material is pulled from a larger, cooler star onto the surface of a much smaller and denser companion. This material builds up until a point is reached when the temperature and pressure at the base of the recently deposited layer are high enough to trigger a nuclear reaction. The material is thrown off into space, resulting in a temporary increase in the light output of the system. We then perceive this increase in brightness as a nova.

OBSERVING VARIABLE STARS

A great number of variable stars are within the reach of amateur instruments, and many can be followed with binoculars. Long period variables are ideal subjects, usually ranging from naked eye visibility down to quite low magnitudes, and needing nothing more elaborate than either binoculars or a small telescope to follow them through their complete cycles of variability. Cepheids are another popular target for the amateur observer, as are the extrinsic variables, whose regular and predictable behaviour make them particularly interesting.

The basic idea behind variable star observation is to compare their brightnesses with those of nearby stars of known magnitude. Although this may sound a somewhat clumsy way of making astronomical observations, you can, with practice, learn to estimate star brightness down to within a tenth of a magnitude! Variable star observation is carried out with the help of a comparison chart which shows the area of sky around the variable. It will include not only the variable itself but other stars of known magnitude in the same area of sky. The long period variable Mira in Cetus makes a good subject for the first-time observer and a comparison chart for Mira can be found in the Northern Autumn/Southern Spring charts.

The comparison stars are used to estimate the brightness of the variable throughout its cycle. This is done by comparing the brightness of the variable at the time of observation to one or more of the comparison stars. This sounds easy, but is more difficult in practice. Yet it is surprising how adept the observer can become at thus estimating magnitudes.

BELOW: Nova Lacerta c1910. The left-hand image shows the nova on 7 August 1907 as a 13th magnitude star prior to its outburst. The centre picture shows the nova as a 7th magnitude object on 31st December 1910, while the right-hand image shows the nova on 29 September 1911 after it had faded to 11th magnitude.

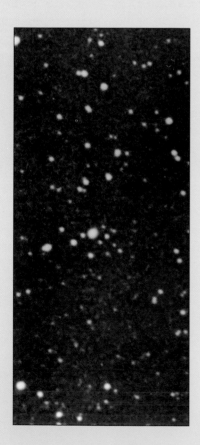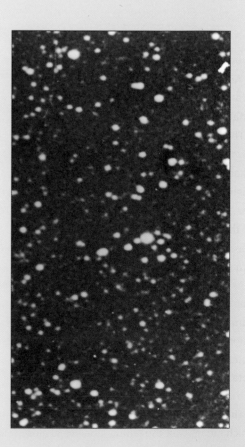

What's in a Name?

Stars and other celestial objects are often identified by catalogue numbers, although a number of the brighter and more conspicuous objects have what are referred to as 'popular' names. Some objects may indeed possess several different names or catalogue numbers, such as the Andromeda Galaxy. This is also known as the M31 (its number in the catalogue of deep sky objects drawn up by the French astronomer Charles Messier in the latter part of the eighteenth century – *see* Appendices), and NGC 224, its classification in the *New General Catalogue of Nebulae and Clusters of Stars* (NGC) prepared by J. L. E. Dreyer and published in 1888. Most star clusters, nebulae and galaxies have designations in either *Messier's Catalogue* or the NGC, although numerous other catalogues do exist. The NGC itself has been supplemented both by the *Index Catalogue* (1895) and the *Second Index Catalogue* (1908).

Naming Stars

Over 200 stars have proper names, of Roman, Greek or Arabic origin. However, only a couple of dozen or so are used regularly, examples of which include Arcturus in Boötes, Spica in Virgo and Betelgeuse in Orion.

The system whereby Greek letters are assigned to stars was introduced by the German astronomer Johann Bayer in 1603. Bayer's system is applied to the brighter stars within any particular constellation, which are given a letter from the Greek alphabet, followed by the genitive case of the constellation in which the star is located. This genitive case is simply the Latin form, meaning 'of' the constellation.

As a rule, the brightest star in a constellation is labelled Alpha, the second brightest Beta, the third Gamma and so on, although there are some constellations where the system falls down. An example is Gemini where the principal star (Pollux) is designated Beta Geminorum, the second brightest (Castor) being known as Alpha Geminorum.

There are only 24 letters in the Greek alphabet, which means that the fainter stars need an alternative system of classification. The system in popular use is that devised by the English Astronomer Royal, John Flamsteed, where the stars in each constellation are listed in order of right ascension. Although many of the brightest stars have both Greek letters and Flamsteed numbers, the latter are generally only used when a star does not have a Greek letter, as is the case with 61 Cygni.

The systems of Bayer and Flamsteed account for most of the brighter stars, fainter stars being identified by their numbers in one of the catalogues used by professional astronomers. These include *Boss's General Catalogue of 33342 Stars* (GC) published in 1937, and the *Smithsonian Astrophysical Observatory Star Catalogue* (SAO), which first appeared in 1966. Typical star designations from these catalogues are GC 15215 and SAO 158687.

DOUBLE AND VARIABLE STAR NOMENCLATURE

Variable stars are assigned Roman capital letters, the sequence starting at R, the letter given to the first variable to be discovered in a constellation. The second discovery is designated S, followed by T and so on through to Z. The sequence then recommences with RR, RS and so on to RZ, then SS to SZ until ZZ is reached. Now a sequence from AA, AB through to AZ is used, followed by BB to BZ and so on through to QZ. The letter J is never used.

After QZ (the 334th variable in a particular constellation) the Roman lettering system is taken over by a somewhat simpler numerical system. From here, variables are designated V335, V336 and so on, this numerical denomination being followed by the genitive form of the constellation name. Bright variable stars which already have Greek letter designations, such as Delta Cephei, are not allocated further numerical designations.

Double stars are usually referred to by their numbers in one of the many double star catalogues, including the *New General Catalogue of Double Stars* (ADS) which was compiled by Aitken in 1932, and the catalogue drawn up by F.G.W. Struve, which utilizes the symbol Σ (the capital form of the Greek letter Sigma) or Σ. Typical designations from these catalogues are ADS 10538 and Σ 2428.

Star Charts

NORTH CIRCUMPOLAR STARS

By far the most prominent and well-known group of stars in this region of sky is the Plough, a pattern formed from the seven brightest stars in the constellation Ursa Major (the Great Bear).

The Plough acts as a useful direction finder to many other stars and constellations, including the leading star in Ursa Minor (the Little Bear), otherwise known as Polaris, or the Pole Star. Extending the line from Merak through Dubhe in the Plough will lead you to Polaris, the nearest star to the North Celestial Pole (*see* 'The Starry Sky').

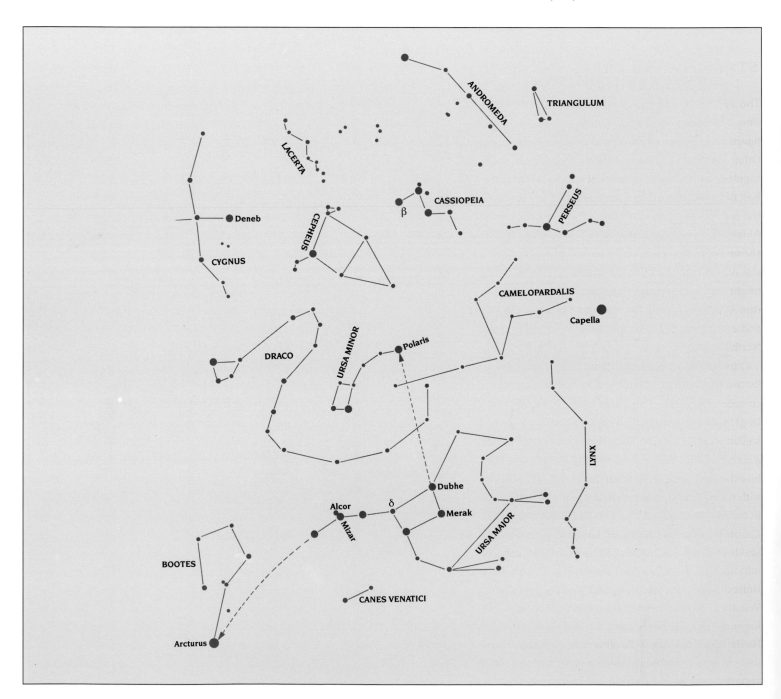

Continuing the line from Merak and Dubhe roughly as far again past Polaris will bring us to Cassiopeia, a prominent W-shaped group of five bright stars. According to legend, Cassiopeia was mother to Princess Andromeda and wife of King Cepheus of Ethiopia, Cepheus being depicted here as one of the constellations adjoining Cassiopeia.

Other groups in this region include Draco (the Dragon), which winds its way around Ursa Minor, and the two obscure groups Camelopardalis (the Giraffe) and Lynx (the Lynx). Very clear skies are needed in order to pick out these latter two groups. Camelopardalis contains no stars brighter than magnitude 4 while Lynx fares little better, containing no star brighter than magnitude 3!

STARS OF NORTHERN WINTER/ SOUTHERN SUMMER

The centrepiece of the constellations visible at this time of year is undoubtedly Orion, a striking celestial figure visible from every inhabited part of the globe. Orion is formed from a rectangle of four bright stars, together with a trio of prominent stars making up the Belt of Orion. This trio of stars points the way to Sirius, the leading star in Canis Major (the Great Dog) and Aldebaran, the brightest star in Taurus (the Bull) as shown here. Sirius is actually the brightest star in the sky. Above and slightly to the east of Aldebaran is the bright star Capella, the leading member of Auriga (the Charioteer), and the sixth brightest star in the entire sky. Capella is also shown on the chart depicting North Circumpolar Stars.

Other prominent groups include Gemini (the Twins), its two leading stars Castor and Pollux forming a conspicuous stellar pair. Procyon in Canis Minor (the Little Dog) is also unmistakable. The long and winding constellation Eridanus (the River Eridanus) stretches from a point just to the northwest of Rigel in Orion down into the southern sky, its meandering form terminating with its leading star Achernar, the ninth brightest star in the sky. The second brightest star in the heavens is Canopus in Carina (the Keel). Canopus lies some 35° south of Sirius and, although hidden to observers at mid-northern latitudes, can be seen from the southern United States. Carina, along with Puppis (the Stern), Vela (the Sail) and Pyxis (the Mariner's Compass), once formed a single, large constellation known as Argo Navis (the Ship Argo). So unwieldy was Argo Navis that it was eventually 'broken up' into the four separate groups now depicted on modern star charts.

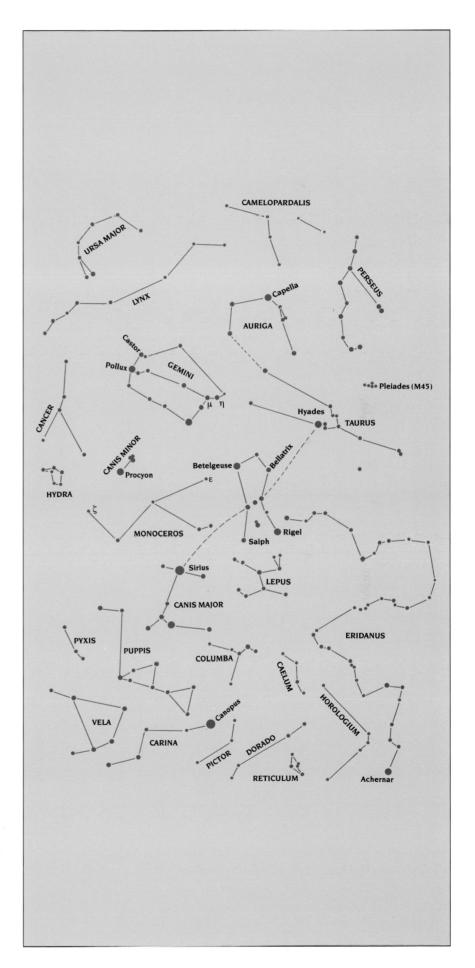

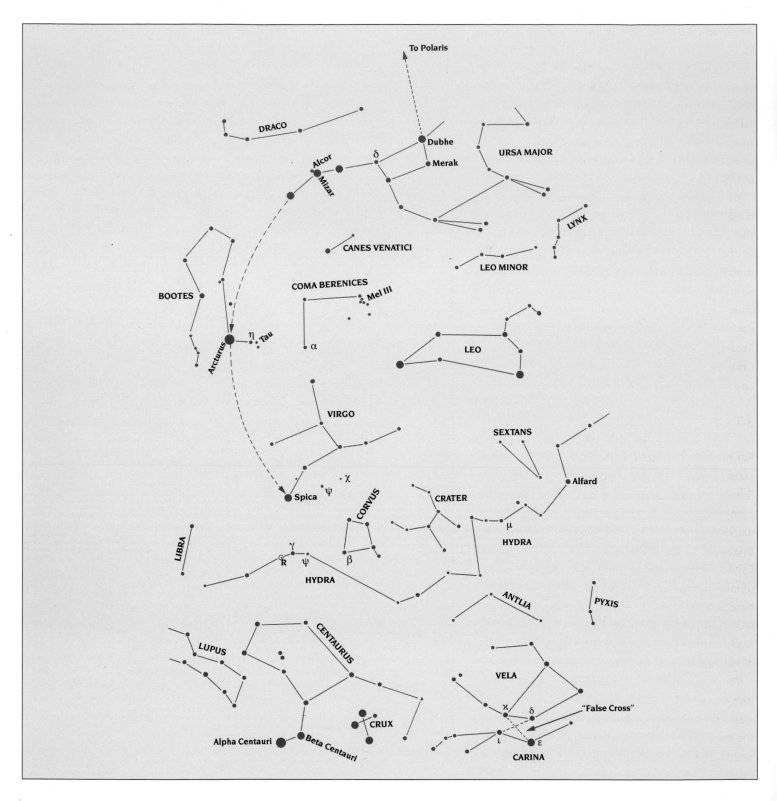

STARS OF NORTHERN SPRING/ SOUTHERN AUTUMN

During northern spring evenings, the seven stars forming the Plough are riding high in the sky for observers at mid-northern latitudes, the curve of stars in the Plough 'handle' leading the way to the bright star Arcturus in Boötes (the Herdsman) as shown here. Arcturus is the fourth brightest star in the sky and its

orangish glow is a lovely sight. Extending the curve as far again brings us to Spica, the sixteenth brightest star to be found in the heavens and the leading star of Virgo (the Virgin).

Leo (the Lion) is one of the few constellations that actually resembles the object or character it is supposed to depict! Another group that can be at least loosely compared to the creature it represents is Hydra (the Water Snake). Hydra is the largest constellation in the sky, and can be seen to stretch all the way across the chart shown here. The Head of Hydra is shown on the chart of Northern Winter/Southern Summer stars (*see* previous page), its long form then taking it to the south of the faint constellation Sextans (the Sextant), Crater (the Cup), Corvus (the Crow), the star Spica in Virgo and to the south-western boundary of Libra (the Scales).

To the south of Hydra can be found some of the most prominent groups in the entire sky. Centaurus (the Centaur) and Crux (the Cross – often referred to as the Southern Cross) can be seen high in the sky during southern autumn by observers at mid-southern latitudes. Not to be confused with Crux are the four stars Kappa and Delta Velorum and Iota and Epsilon Carinae which together make up the famous 'False Cross'. Although the shape is roughly the same as Crux, the stars in the False Cross are somewhat fainter and the difference soon becomes evident.

STARS OF NORTHERN SUMMER/ SOUTHERN WINTER

For northern hemisphere observers, the three bright stars Vega, Deneb and Altair form the conspicuous Summer Triangle. Vega is the leading star of Lyra (the Lyre) and is the fifth brightest star in the sky. Deneb marks the tail of Cygnus (the Swan) while Altair is the brightest star in Aquila (the Eagle). Accompanying Cygnus and Aquila are the tiny constellations Delphinus (the Dolphin) and Sagitta (the Arrow). Also here is the faint group Vulpecula (the Fox), a constellation which is difficult to locate unless the sky is really dark and clear, and whose brightest star is only of magnitude 4.44.

The quadrilateral of stars forming the Head of Draco (the Dragon) is located around 10° to the north-north-west of Vega, while to the west of Vega can be seen the sprawling constellation of Hercules, closely attended by the conspicuous circlet of stars forming Corona Borealis (the Northern Crown).

Corona Australis (the Southern Crown) appears on this chart, a little way to the south of Sagittarius (the Archer) and to the east of the sting of Scorpius (the Scorpion). The brightest star in Scorpius is Antares ('Rival of Mars'). Antares, the fifteenth brightest star in the sky, has a strong ruddy hue, very similar to that of the Red Planet. When Mars is in the same region of sky as Antares the two objects certainly do seem to compete for the attentions of the back-yard stargazer!

Corona Australis is not quite as conspicuous as its northern counterpart, and is typical of several somewhat obscure groups found in the same area of sky, including Microscopium (the Microscope), Indus (the Indian) and Telescopium (the Telescope). Further to the west are the constellations Ara (the Altar) and Norma (the Level). These two groups play host to many star clusters, some of which are described in the detailed charts of Northern Summer/Southern Winter stars.

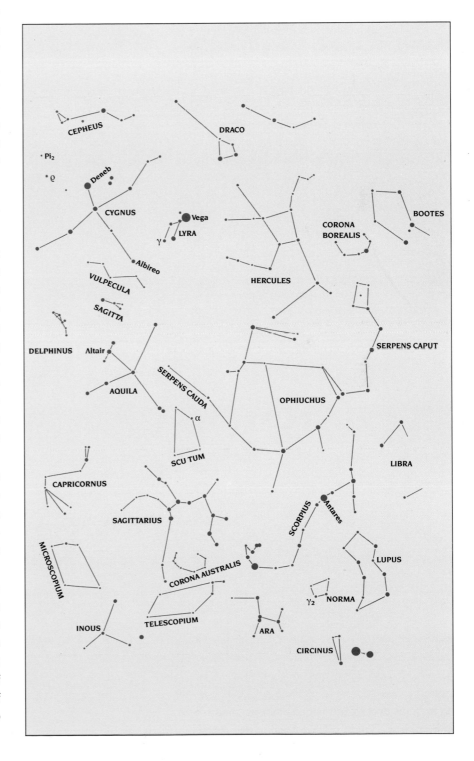

STARS OF NORTHERN AUTUMN/ SOUTHERN SPRING

The Square of Pegasus is one of the dominating features of the autumn sky for northern hemisphere observers. From the Square, the rest of the constellation depicting the legendary winged horse can be made out stretching to the west. Clear skies will reveal tiny Equuleus (the Foal) west of Epsilon Pegasi.

The line of stars forming Andromeda extends from the north-eastern corner of the Square to nearby Perseus, while to the south of Andromeda we see the two small groups Triangulum (the Triangle) and Aries (the Ram). The winding collection of stars forming Pisces (the Fishes) stretches from just south of Beta Andromedae to the southern borders of Pegasus.

Looking a little further to the south, we see the large but somewhat obscure constellation Cetus (the Whale) adjoined on its western borders by Aquarius (the Water Carrier). Extending the line from Beta through Alpha Pegasi down towards the southern horizon will lead to the bright star Fomalhaut in the constellation Piscis Austrinus (the Southern Fish). Fomalhaut is the eighteenth brightest star in the heavens and is the most southerly of the bright stars visible from mid-northern latitudes. This star is often referred to as 'The Solitary One', as there are no other stars of comparable brightness in this area of sky.

To the south of Piscis Austrinus is the prominent constellation Grus (the Crane), adjoining which are two more heavenly birds – Phoenix (the Phoenix) and Tucana (the Toucan) – while the bright star Archernar, marking the end of the trailing constellation Eridanus (the River Eridanus) can be found immediately to the south of Phoenix.

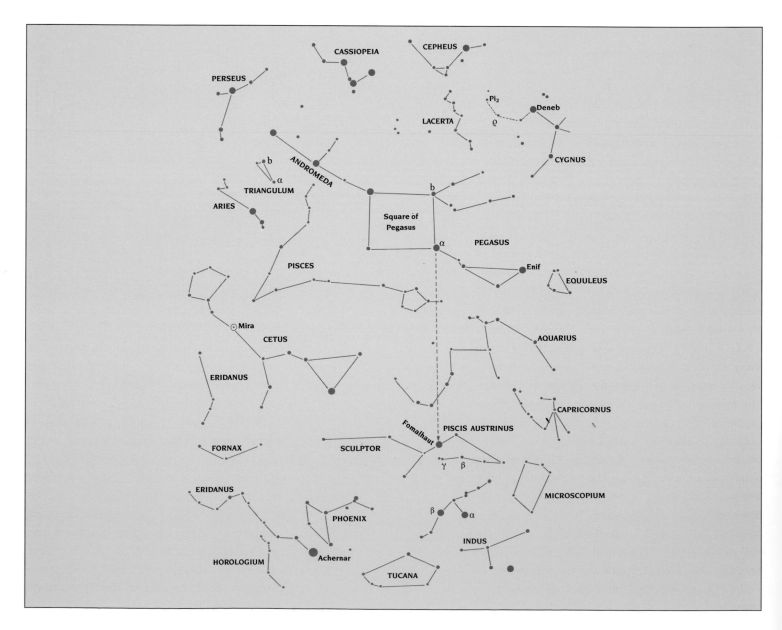

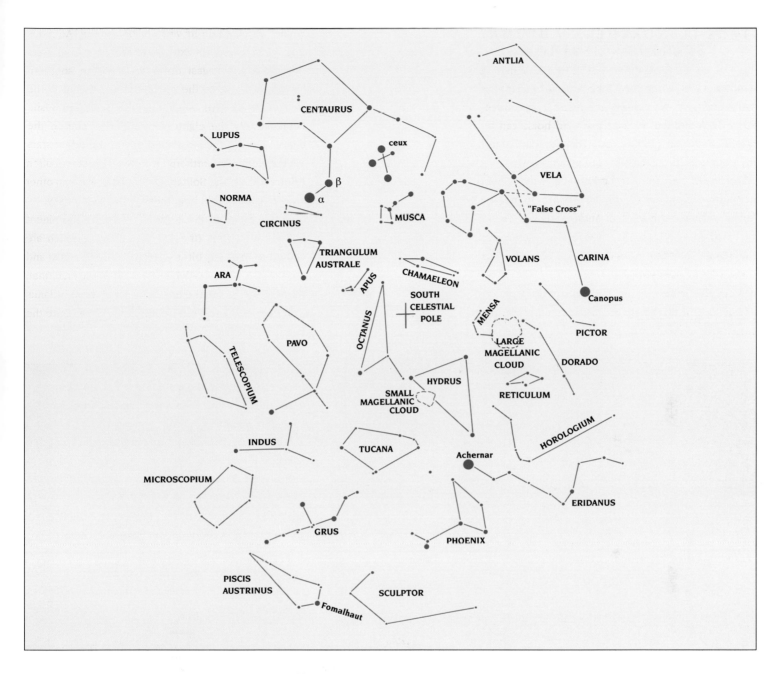

SOUTH CIRCUMPOLAR STARS

Many of the groups in this region of sky are rather faint, including Hydrus (the Little Water Snake), Tucana (the Toucan) and Octans (the Octant). This latter group contains the South Celestial Pole. Unlike its northern counterpart, there is no really bright star marking the polar position. The nearest naked eye star to this point is Sigma Octantis (not shown here) which lies within 1° of the South Celestial Pole. Sigma is sometimes referred to as the 'Southern Polaris', although at magnitude 5.46 it hardly rivals the true Polaris located 180° to the north in Ursa Minor! Very clear skies are needed to see Sigma Octantis with the naked eye.

The constellation Crux (the Cross) can be used to locate the position of the South Celestial Pole, its longer arm pointing in its direction. Another way of determining its position is to locate the Large and Small Magellanic Clouds which form a right angled triangle with the pole. Both these galaxies (described more fully with the detailed charts of South Circumpolar Stars) are visible to the naked eye even under moonlit conditions.

In spite of this area containing mainly faint and sometimes obscure groups, the region is ringed by the bright stars Alpha and Beta Centauri in Centaurus (the Centaur), Canopus in Carina (the Keel) and Achernar in Eridanus (the River Eridanus). Using these stars as a framework, and armed with the accompanying chart, you should be able to identify the south circumpolar constellations.

DETAILED CHART FOR NORTH CIRCUMPOLAR STARS
M52 Open Cluster

Cassiopeia lies within the Milky Way and contains a number of open star clusters accessible to binoculars or small telescopes. One of these is M52 (NGC 7654), a group of around a hundred stars located just to the

BELOW: *Finder chart for M52 open cluster. Beta Cassiopeias identified on page 42.*

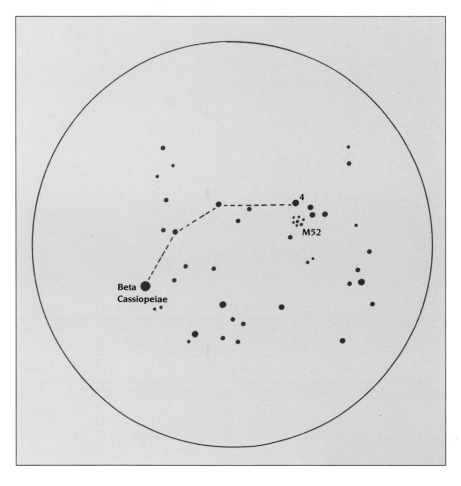

Alcor, Mizar and Sidus Ludovicianum

Ursa Major, the Great Bear, is probably the most famous and well-known constellation in the entire sky. Although most of the group is comprised of relatively faint stars, the seven brightest stars within the constellation make up the Plough. This region of sky contains several objects of interest to the observer using binoculars or a small telescope.

The central star in the Plough 'handle' is magnitude 2.4 Mizar, which has a companion located immediately to its east. This companion is Alcor which at magnitude 4, is an easy naked eye object. Those with keen eyesight will be able to resolve the Alcor/Mizar pair which lie 11.8′ apart.

Mizar itself is a double star, the first double star to be discovered with a telescope. The discovery was made by the Italian astronomer Giovanni Battista Riccioli in around 1650. Small telescopes will reveal Mizar's magnitude 4 companion which lies just 14.4″ away; together they form a notable pair when seen in a small telescope.

Located between Alcor and Mizar, a little to the south of a line joining the two stars, is the 8th magnitude star Sidus Ludovicianum, observed by the German astronomer and mathematician J. G. Liebknecht in December 1722. Liebknecht carried out a series of observations of this star and came to the conclusion that it was in motion. This led him to the decision that the object was in fact a new planet, and he promptly gave it its unusual name, in honour of his sovereign the Landgrave Ludwig of Hessen-Darmstadt.

FACING PAGE, BELOW: *Wide field view showing the conspicuous shape of the Plough (bottom) together with Ursa Minor and its leading star Polaris just above centre.*

RIGHT: *Open cluster M52 (NGC 7654) in Cassipeia. Lying at a distance of around 4,500 light-years, M52 has a diameter of between 10 and 15 light-years.*

south of the star 4 Cassiopeiae, the latter easily found by star hopping from Beta Cassiopeiae as shown on the accompanying chart.

M52 has a magnitude of 6.9 and lies at a distance of just over 5,000 light-years. It can be seen through binoculars as a small, diffuse patch of light with several individual stars resolved. Telescopes reveal many more stars in the cluster which has an apparent diameter of 13′, making it over a third the diameter of the Moon's disc.

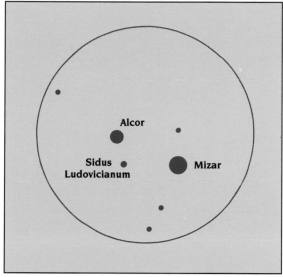

ABOVE/LEFT: *Identification chart and photograph for Alcor, Mizar and Sidus* *Ludovicianum. Alcor and Mizar are identified on pages 42 and 44.*

Liebknecht's enthusiasm was short-lived, however! Following the announcement, several other astronomers observed the 'new planet', all coming to the correct conclusion that it was nothing more dramatic than an ordinary faint star! Liebknecht came in for some severe criticism from a number of his contemporaries who cast grave doubts on his abilities as an observer. Nonetheless the unusual name given to the star by Liebknecht was retained. Sidus Ludovicianum is one of the faintest stars in the sky to possess a name other than a catalogue number, which in itself makes it of interest to the backyard astronomer!

The Plough and Ursa Minor (wide field view)

This spectacular wide field view shows the seven brightest stars of Ursa Major (The Great Bear) forming the conspicuous and well-known shape of the Plough, or Big Dipper, at the bottom of the picture. Extending the line between the two end stars of the 'bowl' of the Plough upwards leads us to Polaris, the brightest star in Ursa Minor (The Little Bear) which marks the position of the North Celestial Pole. The rest of Ursa Minor can be seen extending away to the lower left of Polaris, collectively resembling a miniature version of the Plough. Ursa Minor is indeed often referred to as 'the Little Dipper'. The two stars at the opposite end of Ursa Minor to Polaris are Kochab (right) and Pherkad. These two stars have been known for centuries as 'the Guardians of the Pole', although Arabic astronomers referred to them as 'the Two Calves'.

Double star M40

M40 is the only object in Messier's catalogue which is of a non-nebular nature, being nothing more than a close pair of faint stars located around 1.5° to the north-east of Delta Ursae Majoris as shown on the accompanying finder chart. Also known as Wcn 4, its reference in the catalogue of double stars compiled by A. Winnecke in 1863, the components of M40 are of magnitudes 9.0 and 9.3 and are separated by 50.1". Both stars are resolvable in small telescopes. The German astronomer Johannes Hevelius actually recorded a nebula at this spot in 1660, this observation being followed up by Messier in 1764 who recorded the object as: '. . . two stars, very close together and of equal brightness . . . situated at the root of the tail of the Great Bear . . . It is presumed that Hevelius mistook these two stars for a nebulae . . .' In spite of the non-nebular status of the object, it nevertheless found its way into Messier's catalogue.

M81 and M82 Galaxies

Ursa Major contains several galaxies, a number of which are well within the reach of amateur telescopes. The best known are undoubtedly M81 (NGC 3031) and M82 (NGC 3034) which are located to the northwest of Merak and Dubhe, the two end stars of the 'bowl' of the Plough.

M81 is a spiral galaxy with a magnitude of 7.9 rendering it just visible in good binoculars on a really clear night. Remember, as with any object of this type, to look for a patch of light rather than a starlike point. To locate M81 and its neighbour M82, starhop your way from Merak, through Dubhe and 38 Ursae Majoris as shown. M81 and M82 lie to either side of a line forming a small triangle of stars with 24 Ursae Majoris at its apex.

M82 is an edge-on galaxy which appears to be irregular in form. The magnitude of M82 is 9.3, somewhat fainter than its neighbour and requiring large binoculars or a telescope to bring it out. Telescopes of 4in (100mm) aperture will show M81 to be an oval-shaped nebulous patch, the same instrument revealing M82 as a cigar-shaped sliver of light with a uniform surface brightness. Larger instruments, of 8in (200mm) aperture or more, will start to bring out some detail in each object. The spiral arms of M81 appear as a disc of faint nebulosity around its brighter central regions when viewed through high powers, while dark patches may also be seen superimposed on the surface of M82.

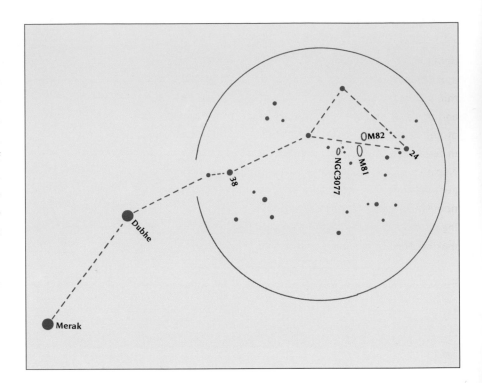

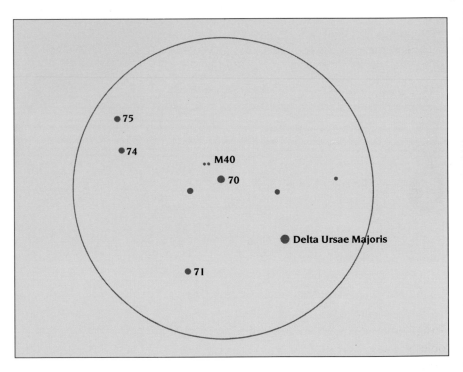

TOP: *Finder chart for double star M40. Delta Ursae Majoris is identified on pages 42 and 44.*

ABOVE: *Finder chart for M81, M82 and NGC 3077 galaxies. Merak and Dubhe are identified on pages 42 and 44.*

M81 and M82 are the leading members of the Ursa Major cluster of galaxies, a group of around a dozen galaxies situated some 7 million light-years away. Another member of the group is 11th magnitude NGC 3077, which forms a small triangle with M81 and M82. This is a dwarf galaxy with a diameter thought to be around 6,000 light-years, somewhat smaller than its neighbours M81 (36,000 light-years) and M82 (16,000 light-years). A 6in (150mm) diameter telescope at low power should show this object.

Photograph of M81 and M82

This negative photograph (right) reveals a wealth of detail in the spiral galaxy M81. The bright nucleus is apparent as are the spiral arms, normally visible through large telescopes of 16in (400mm) aperture and upwards, smaller telescopes showing only a disc of nebulosity surrounding the nucleus. Irregularities in the edges of cigar-shaped M82 can also be seen. Negative photographs like the one reproduced here generally offer a better contrast between objects like nebulae and galaxies and the surrounding sky, bringing out subtle details that may well be impossible to make out in an ordinary 'positive' photograph.

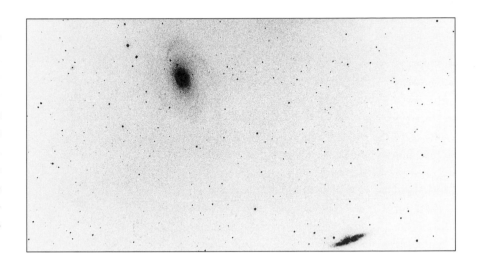

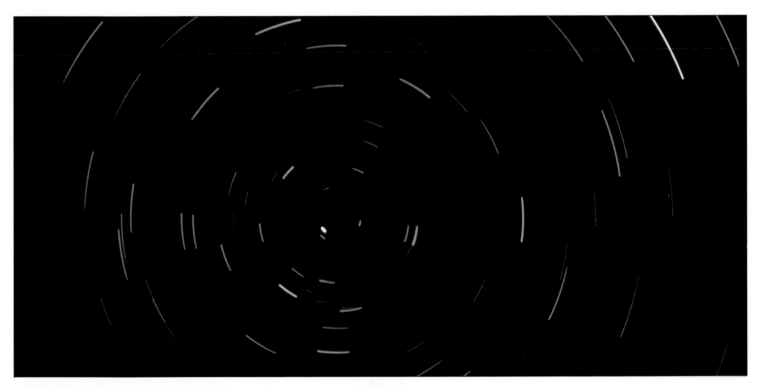

Star trails around the north celestial pole

The apparent motion of the stars and other celestial objects from east to west through the sky is due to the actual rotation of the Earth from west to east. The result of the Earth's axial rotation is that the celestial sphere appears to move around the Earth, stars seeming to rise in the east, travelling across the sky and setting in the west.

The Earth's axis of rotation is pointed towards two locations on the celestial sphere. These points are known as the north and south celestial poles, and all the stars in the sky appear to rotate around these points. This apparent circumpolar motion is well illustrated in the above photograph.

TOP: *Galaxies M81 (top) and M82 in Ursa Major.*

ABOVE: *Star trails around the North Celestial Pole. The short, bright star trail at centre is Polaris.*

The bright star near centre of the picture is Polaris. Also known as the Pole Star, this is the closest naked-eye star to the north celestial pole. To obtain the effect seen here, the camera shutter has been left open for an hour.

Polaris hardly appears to have moved at all, because it is almost at the centre of rotation. However, the further away we come from this point, the larger are the arcs described by the star trails. These star trails are caused as the star images have moved across the field of view of the camera. Had the camera been attached to an equatorial mounting (*see* page 11) and set to follow the stars as they crossed the sky, they would have been recorded as points of light on the final picture.

DETAILED CHARTS FOR NORTHERN WINTER/ SOUTHERN SUMMER

M35 open star cluster

One of the most easily observed open star clusters using binoculars or small telescopes is M35 (NGC 2168) in Gemini. With a magnitude of 5.3, M35 is easy to locate, lying at the north-western corner of Gemini at the end of the line of stars formed from Mu, Eta, 6, 4 and 3 Geminorum. If the sky is really dark and clear you may be able to glimpse M35 with the naked eye. This cluster lies at a distance of around 2,200 light-years and contains around 120 stars. It has an apparent diameter of around 35', similar to that of the lunar disc, and 7×50 binoculars, with their very wide field of view, are ideally suited to this object. Its apparent diameter is so large that the normally narrower fields of view given by telescopes show only its inner regions.

Roughly half a degree to the south-west of M35 is the much smaller and fainter open cluster NGC 2158. This object contains around 150 stars although it is so far away, at a distance of around 16,000 light-years, that their total combined magnitude is only 11.6. A little brighter is the open cluster NGC 2129, situated

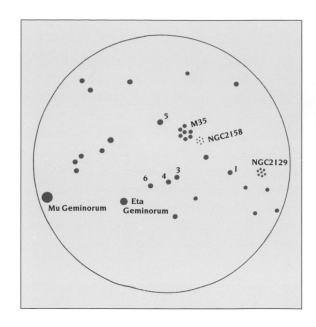

R I G H T: Finder chart for M35, IC 2158 and NGC 2129 open star clusters. Mu, Eta and 1 Geminorum are identified on page 43.

B E L O W: The open cluster M35 in Gemini has a diameter of around 30 light-years and a total luminosity some 2,500 times that of the Sun.

somewhat further to the south-west. NGC 2129 has a magnitude of 6.7 and contains around 40 stars. Telescopes of 6in (150mm) aperture or larger will resolve quite a number of the individual stars within this cluster, smaller telescopes revealing just its brighter members. Binoculars show NGC 2129 as a small nebulous patch of light.

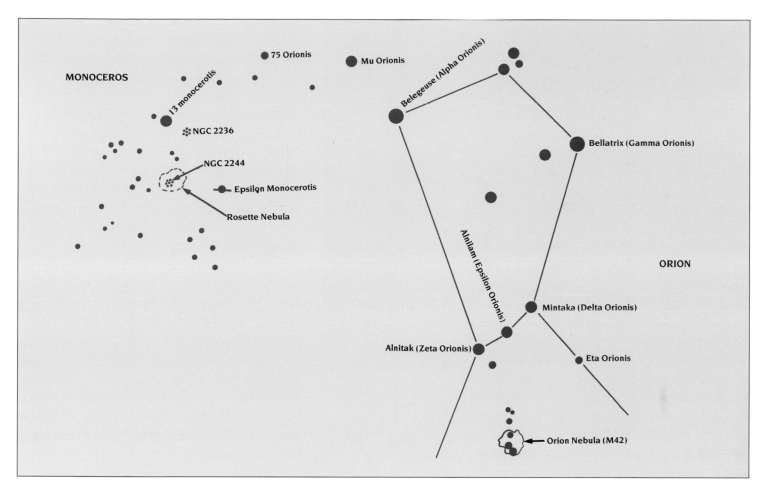

MONOCEROS

75 Orionis

13 monocerotis

NGC 2236

NGC 2244

Epsilon Monocerotis

Rosette Nebula

Mu Orionis

Belegeuse (Alpha Orionis)

Bellatrix (Gamma Orionis)

Alnilam (Epsilon Orionis)

ORION

Mintaka (Delta Orionis)

Alnitak (Zeta Orionis)

Eta Orionis

Orion Nebula (M42)

Monoceros

Although the constellation Monoceros (the Unicorn) contains no stars above magnitude 3.7, it lies across the Milky Way; what it lacks in bright stars it more than makes up for with rich star fields and open star clusters. The whole area is well worth sweeping either with binoculars or a wide field telescope.

Two of these clusters are described here. To locate NGC 2236, follow the line of stars Betelgeuse, Mu and 75 Orionis until you reach 13 Monocerotis as shown. NGC 2236, a collection of around 50 stars with a combined magnitude of 8.5, lies a little way to the southwest of 13 Monocerotis. It is a challenge for binocular observers who may pick the cluster out as a small diffuse patch of nebulosity, although small telescopes may resolve one or two member stars. NGC 2236 shines from a distance of over 10,000 light-years.

One of the most remarkable objects in Monoceros is the Rosette Nebula, also known as NGC 2237, NGC 2238, NGC 2239 and NGC 2246, different numbers being given to different regions of the nebula. The Rosette Nebula is located a couple of degrees to the south of NGC 2236. Searching the area with binoculars will initially reveal the open cluster NGC 2244. Shining

ABOVE: *The region of sky including Monoceros and northern Orion. Betelgeuse, Bellatrix and Epsilon Monocerotis are identified on page 43.*

from a distance of around 5,500 light-years, the 100 or so stars in NGC 2244 have a combined magnitude of 4.8, making the cluster dimly visible to the naked eye on clear, dark nights. Binoculars bring out several cluster stars while a 6in (150mm) aperture telescope will bring out several dozen.

The NGC 2244 cluster is quite young by cosmic standards, thought by astronomers to be only around three million years old. As with other clusters, NGC 2244 formed through the gravitational collapse of a huge interstellar gas cloud, or nebula. Portions of this cloud, the remnants of which are visible today as the Rosette Nebula, collapsed to form clumps which continued to gather up more and more of the surrounding gas. Eventually the clumps became of sufficient size to produce very high internal pressures and temperatures. These conditions instigated thermonuclear reactions, similar to those inside our own Sun, following which the stars in NGC 2244 began to shine.

Young stars such as those in NGC 2244 are extremely hot, and give out copious amounts of ultraviolet energy. This energy is absorbed by the gas in the nebula which in turn emits visible light. Nebulae of this type are referred to as emisson nebulae. Some-

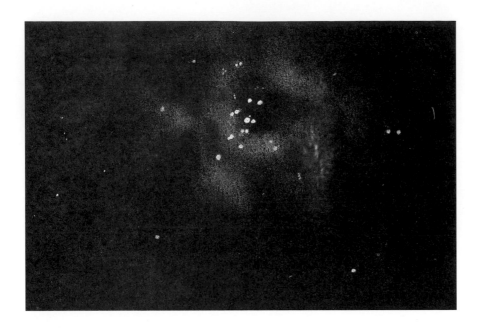

times nebulae are found near stars which are not hot enough to actually cause the gas to shine. These clouds, known as reflection nebulae, are rendered visible through the reflection of starlight. The third type, dark nebulae, are clouds of gas and dust which contain no stars whatsoever and block out the light from more distant stars. One of the best known dark

ABOVE: *Drawing of the Rosette Nebula in Monoceros as seen through a 12-inch (300 mm) reflector.*

BELOW: *The Great Nebula (M42) in Orion.*

nebulae is the Coal Sack, a vast cloud of obscuring material in the constellation of Crux. A photograph of the Coal Sack, once believed to be a hole in the Milky Way, appears in the section covering South Circumpolar Stars (*see* page 47).

Although some observers have glimpsed the Rosette Nebula through binoculars, it is very difficult to see this way, and telescopes of at least 6in (150mm) aperture are usually needed to bring out its pearly glow. Located 2½° to the west of the Rosette Nebula is the double star Epsilon Monocerotis, its magnitude 4.5 and 6.5 components separated by 13.4″, making it an easy object for small telescopes.

The Orion Nebula

Before leaving this region, we must take a closer look at one of the most splendid deep sky objects in the entire heavens. The Orion Nebula (M42), located to the south of the three stars that form the Belt of Orion, is visible to the naked eye as a shimmering patch of light. The constellation of Orion (the Hunter) straddles the celestial equator and is visible from most locations on the globe, as is Monoceros described above. Both groups are best placed for observation

during evenings in December, January and February. From mid-northern latitudes Orion is seen high over the southern horizon, whilst from the equatorial regions he can be seen passing overhead. Observers in mid-southern latitudes see Orion well up in the northern sky.

The Orion Nebula is a vast cloud of interstellar gas located in the line of stars marking the Sword of Orion. Visible as a greenish misty patch through small telescopes, this fine object is usually one of the first to which amateur astronomers turn their gaze. It was the first nebula to be photographed successfully, by the American astronomer Henry Draper in 1880. It lies at a distance of around 1,600 light-years, and the bright central region normally captured on photographs has a true diameter of some 30 light-years. The overall magnitude is around 3.5, its glow being caused, as is the case with other emission nebulae, by the emission of visible light following the absorption of strong ultraviolet radiation from the young, hot stars embedded within it.

Another object of note in Orion is the double star Delta Orionis, or Mintaka, the westernmost star in the Belt of Orion. Mintaka has white and bluish components of magnitudes 2.2 and 6.7 separated by 52.8", making it an easy object for small telescopes.

The Belt and Sword of Orion and the Orion Nebula

This photograph at right shows the Belt of Orion, made up of Alnitak (Zeta Orionis), Alnilam (Epsilon Orionis) and Mintaka (Delta Orionis), together with Orion's Sword to the south (below). The Orion Nebula is clearly visible. Rigel (Beta Orionis), the bright star to the south-west (lower right) of picture is the brightest star in Orion and the seventh brightest star in the sky. It is also a double star, although the glare of the brightest component (magnitude 0.1) blots out the faint glow from its magnitude 6.8 companion. A telescope of at least 4in (100mm) aperture is required to resolve this pair which are separated by 9.5". Even then you may have difficulty in seeing the light from the bluish companion as it struggles to make its presence felt in the glare of the white primary star!

Eta Orionis, the bright star below and right of Mintaka, is another double star. Its white components are of magnitudes 3.8 and 4.8 and are separated by just 1.5". A telescope of at least 6in (150mm) aperture is needed in order to resolve this close pair. A third component of magnitude 9.4 may be seen 115.1" away.

B E L O W: *The Belt of Orion can be seen near the top of the picture with the Sword of Orion visible to the south (below). The Orion Nebula (M42) is clearly visible as a glowing patch in the Sword.*

Alnitak is another double with components of magnitudes 1.9 and 4.0 separated by 2.6". Again there is a third star, this being magnitude 9.9 and lying 57.6" away. The two main stars are white and are resolved with a telescope of 4in (100mm) aperture, which should also bring out the third, fainter member of this system.

DETAILED CHARTS FOR NORTHERN SPRING/ SOUTHERN SUMMER

Sombrero Hat Galaxy M104 (NGC 4594) in Virgo

The constellation of Virgo contains a large number of galaxies, many of which are visible in small to medium-sized telescopes. The reason is that this area of sky is home to the Virgo Cluster of Galaxies, a huge collection of island universes some 60 million light-years away. The Virgo Cluster lies at the heart of the Local Supercluster, a vast assemblage of galaxies and clusters of galaxies of which the Local Group and our own Milky Way Galaxy are distant members.

M104 (NGC 4594) is the brightest of the galaxies in Virgo. It shines with an overall magnitude of 8.3 and is a popular target for the backyard observer. It is quite easy to locate, lying on one of the sides of the triangle formed from the stars Psi and Chi Virginis and Σ 1669 as shown on the accompanying chart (right).

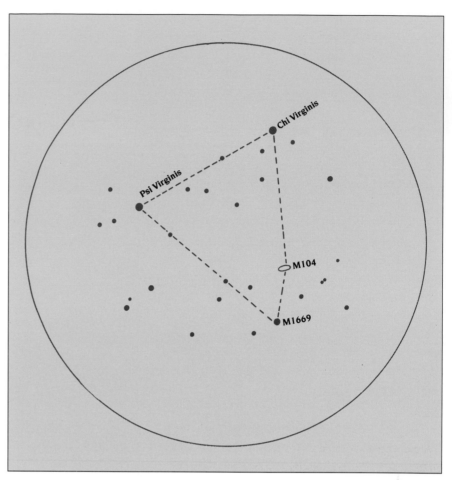

ABOVE: *Finder chart for M104 spiral galaxy. Psi and Chi Virginis are identified on page 44.*

LEFT: *Drawing of M104 spiral galaxy as seen through a 12-inch (300 mm) reflector.*

M53 globular cluster and M64 'Black Eye' Galaxy

One of the brightest stars in the northern spring night sky is Arcturus, or Alpha Boötis. Arcturus, together with nearby Eta and Tau Boötis, can be used as direction finders to the nearby and much less conspicuous constellation of Coma Berenices. This group of stars lies to the north of Virgo and contains a number of galaxies belonging to the Virgo Cluster of Galaxies.

RIGHT: *Drawing of M64 spiral galaxy as seen through a 12-inch (300 mm) reflector.*

The Sombrero Hat Galaxy, as M104 is popularly known, got its name from the dark dust lane seen to cut across it. The galaxy is virtually edge-on to us and we see little if anything of its spiral form. When seen through a small telescope M104 appears as little more than an elongated smudge of light, although larger instruments give a better indication of its actual shape. The dust band can be seen with a 12in (300mm) telescope providing the sky is really dark and clear.

Σ 1669 is a triple star with magnitude 6.0 and 6.1 components lying 5.4″ apart. The third star, shining with a magnitude of 10.5, lies 59.0″ away from these. Although a small telescope will resolve the two main components, the third member of this system may just be glimpsed through a 3in (75mm) telescope.

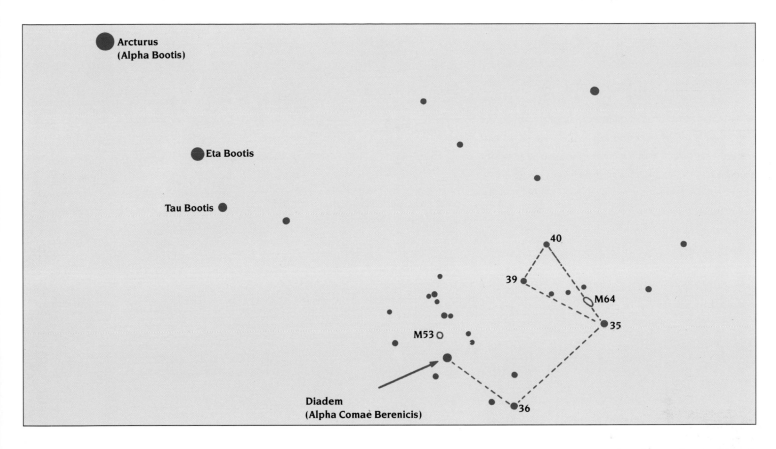

Arcturus
(Alpha Bootis)

Eta Bootis

Tau Bootis

40

39

M64

35

M53 ○

Diadem
(Alpha Comaè Berenicis)

36

Alpha Comae Berenicis, also known as Diadem, lies quite close to the magnitude 7.7 globular cluster M53 (NGC 5024), easily located just 1° to the north-east of Diadem. M53 lies at a distance of around 60,000 light-years and, like other globular clusters, is a huge spherical collection of stars. Globular clusters can have diameters of anything up to several hundred light-years, within which region there can be upwards of several tens of thousands of stars. Unlike open clusters, which are found within the spiral arms of our Galaxy (and other galaxies) and which orbit the galactic centre in more or less circular paths, globulars are found within a huge volume of space known as the galactic halo. This is a colossal gathering of stars (most of which are members of globular clusters) which completely surrounds the central bulge of our Galaxy. Globular clusters travel around the galactic centre in elliptical paths. M53 can be picked up quite easily in binoculars, although telescopes are required to resolve any of its individual members.

A few degrees to the north-north-west of Diadem is the triangle of stars formed from 35, 39 and 40 Comae Berenicis. Located roughly 1° along the line from 35 to 40 is the famous Black Eye Galaxy, or M64 (NGC 4826) M64 got its unusual name from the large patch of obscuring dust seen silhouetted against its face when viewed through telescopes. As far as binoculars are

ABOVE: Location chart for M53 globular cluster and M64 spiral galaxy. Arcturus, Eta and Tau Bootis and Alpha Comae Berenicis are identified on page 44.

BELOW RIGHT: The Coma Berenices star cluster, a conspicuous scattering of naked eye stars and (at 250 light years) one of the nearest open star clusters.

concerned, M64 is a somewhat elusive object, although at magnitude 8.6 it can just be glimpsed under clear, dark skies. A 4in (100mm) telescope will show the general shape of the galaxy quite well, although a 6in (150mm) instrument is needed in order to reveal its dark patch. M64 lies at a distance of between 20 and 25 million light-years.

Coma Berenices open star cluster

The northern regions of Coma Berenices are dominated by the large open cluster Mel III, its reference in the catalogue drawn up by astronomer P. J. Melotte in the early part of this century. Also known as the Coma Cluster, Mell III is shown on the chart on page 44. It has an apparent diameter of around 6°, slightly

larger than the distance between the two end stars in the 'bowl' of the Plough, seen 25° further to the north. It lies at a distance of some 250 light-years, making it one of the closest known open star clusters. Some three dozen or more stars have been identified as being true members of the cluster. As far as observing this group is concerned, the best views are to be had through binoculars, which will show most of the cluster at one go. The much smaller fields of view given by the telescopes will only show a small section of the cluster at any one time. The overall magnitude of Mell III is around 3.

FACING PAGE, TOP LEFT: *Drawing of M68 globular cluster as seen through a 12-inch (300 mm) reflector.*

BELOW: *Chart of Hydra and Corvus.*

BOTTOM: *Finder charter for M48 open cluster. Zeta Monocerotis is identified on page 43.*

as a large, dim patch almost twice the diameter of the lunar disc. However, telescopes are required in order to bring out some of this cluster's individual member stars.

Identifying the quadrilateral of stars that form the constellation Corvus the Crow will help you to locate M68 (NGC 4590) which, as the finder charts below and right show, lies a little to the south-south-east of Beta Corvi. M68 shines with a magnitude of 3.2 and lies at a distance of around 30,000 light-years. M68 was discovered by the French astronomer Charles Messier in 1780. It can be glimpsed in binoculars, appearing as a

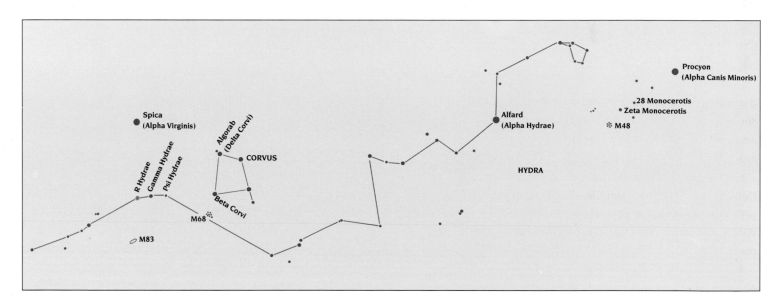

Hydra

The long and sprawling constellation Hydra (the Water Snake) is the largest constellation in the heavens, its winding form occupying a larger area of the celestial sphere than any other group. Hydra can be seen from most areas of the world and is best placed for observation during spring in the northern hemisphere and autumn in the south.

The Head of Hydra can be found a short way to the east of the bright star Procyon in Canis Minor. From here, the heavenly snake winds its way south of Sextans, Crater, Corvus and the bright star Spica in Virgo to end up near Libra. Its leading star, Alfard, has a magnitude of 1.98, no other star within the group exceeding magnitude 3. However, Hydra contains a number of interesting objects well worth seeking out.

First port of call is the open cluster M48 (NGC 2548), a magnitude 5.8 gathering of around 80 stars visible 4° to the south-east of nearby Zeta Monocerotis (see finder chart, right). M48 lies at a distance of around 2,000 light-years and can be seen through binoculars

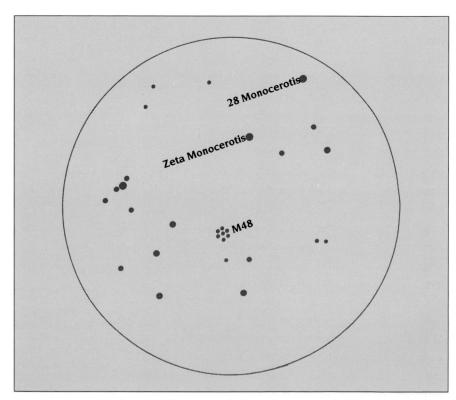

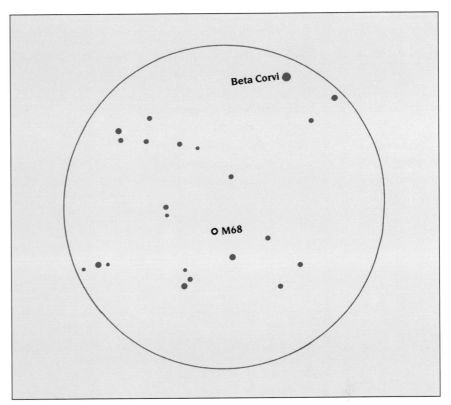

decidedly non-stellar object, although telescopes of 8in (200mm) diameter and upwards will reveal large numbers of individual components of this cluster, presenting a fine spectacle under crisp, dark skies.

Moving out of Hydra for the moment we come to Delta Corvi, or Algorab, a double star with whitish and yellowish components of magnitudes 3.0 and 9.2. With a separation of 24.2″, these two stars can be resolved in small telescopes.

M83 (NGC 5236) is a spiral galaxy shining at magnitude 8.2 and located roughly 18° due south of Spica. This is the brightest galaxy in Hydra and can be seen through binoculars as a fairly conspicuous circular patch of nebulosity, roughly a third the diameter of the lunar disc. M83 is a face-on spiral galaxy whose small nucleus becomes readily visible in telescopes of 8in (200mm) diameter and upwards. This huge system has a diameter of around 30,000 light-years, roughly the distance between ourselves and the globular M68 (described above), and lies at a distance of some 10 million light-years. It can be located by using the finder chart at right and star hopping south from the trio of stars R, Gamma and Psi Hydrae.

R Hydrae is an interesting object in its own right. Here we have a long period variable star whose brightness varies between 4th and 10th magnitude over a period of 386 days. It is of similar type to Mira, or Omicron Ceti (see page 64) and was the third variable of its type to be discovered. Its complete cycle of variability can be seen through good binoculars or a small telescope and it is in fact one of the easiest of the long period variables to be observed by amateur astronomers. For a few weeks around maximum R

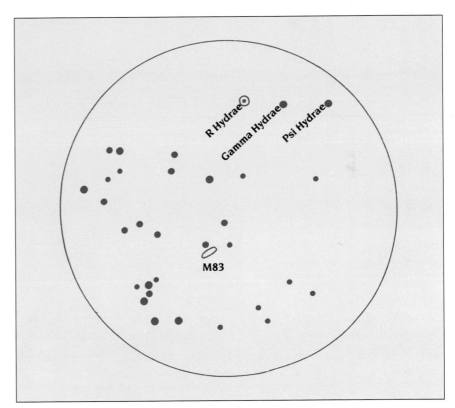

TOP: Finder chart for M68 globular cluster. Beta Corvi identified is on page 44.

ABOVE: Finder chart for M83 spiral galaxy. R, Gamma and Psi Hydrae are identified on page 44.

Hydrae can be seen with the naked eye. If you look for R Hydrae and have difficulty spotting it, the star may well be at or near its minimum brightness. Keeping a regular watch on the area will eventually reap its rewards as the star reappears during its climb back to maximum magnitude.

DETAILED CHARTS FOR NORTHERN SUMMER/ SOUTHERN WINTER

M26 and NGC 6664 open clusters

Lying almost 1° to the east-south-east of Delta Scuti, and visible through binoculars as a small nebulous patch, M26 (NGC 6694) is situated against an impressive backdrop of the Milky Way. This is a fairly easy object for small telescopes, which reveal the group as a small, compact collection of stars. M26 lies at a distance of around 4,900 light-years and contains around 30 stars, shining with a combined magnitude of 8. However, only the dozen or so brightest of these can be seen with small instruments.

Lying in the same field as M26, close to Alpha Scuti, is the magnitude 7.8 open cluster NGC 6664. This object is somewhat closer than M26, shining from a distance of just over 4,000 light-years. It contains around 50 stars and is best viewed with low power eyepieces which take in the whole cluster comfortably.

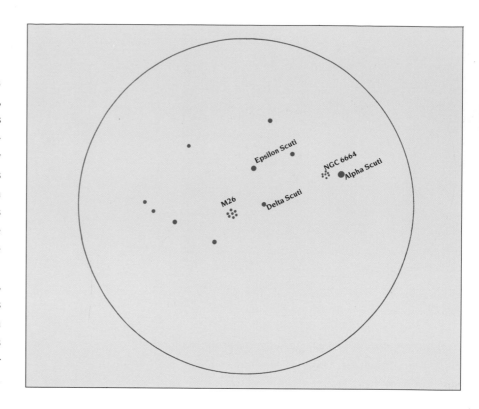

M39 open cluster

The bright open cluster M39 (NGC 7092) in Cygnus is one of the showpieces of the summer night sky. With a combined magnitude of 4.6, M39 contains around 30 stars and shines from a distance of around 800 light-years. It is a fairly scattered collection, being described as a 'rather splashy galaxy field of stars' by the English astronomer Admiral William Henry Smyth. Best viewed with a low power eyepiece, M39 is easily found at the

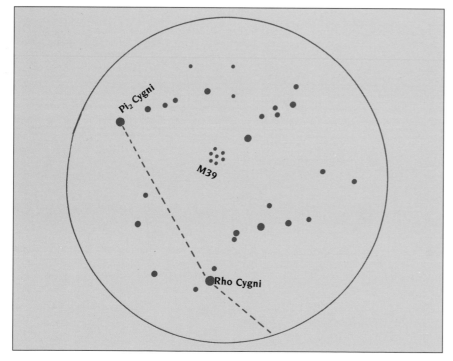

end of a circlet of stars extending to the east of Deneb. Binoculars bring out the group very well, revealing several individual member stars and the conspicuous wedge-shape form of the cluster.

TOP: Finder chart for M26 and NGC 6664 open clusters. Alpha Scuti is identified on page 45.

ABOVE LEFT Finder chart for M39 open cluster. Rho and Pi₂ Cygni are identified on pages 45 and 46.

ABOVE RIGHT: Globular cluster M56 in Lyra.

M56 globular cluster

Located in the south-eastern region of Lyra, M56 (NGC 6779) is a magnitude 8.3 globular cluster found roughly midway between Gamma Lyrae and Albireo (Beta Cygni). Binoculars and small telescopes show M56 as a small, diffuse starlike object, larger instruments being needed in order to bring out any individual member stars. M56 shines from a distance of over 30,000 light-years.

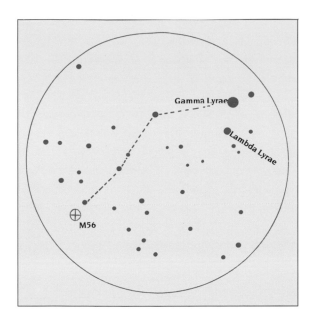

Lyra/Head of Draco centred near Vega

This view at right shows the small but conspicuous constellation of Lyra, the Lyre, its brilliant leading star Vega visible just below and to the right of centre. With a magnitude of 0.04, Vega is the fifth brightest star in the entire sky and shines from a distance of 27 light-years.

Lyra plays host to a number of double stars, one of which is Beta Lyrae, the star furthest to the west (right) of the quadrilateral of stars visible just below Vega. The brightest component of Beta Lyrae is actually the prototype of the Beta Lyrae class of eclipsing variables. These stars have components which are so close together that they become distorted into elliptical shapes through their combined gravitational attraction. The light variations of Beta Lyrae, as with all variables of its type, are continuous. Beta Lyrae varies between magnitudes 3.3 and 4.3 over a period of 12.94 days. The secondary star in the Beta Lyrae double system has a magnitude of 8.6, the two components being separated by 45.7″.

One of the most famous objects in Lyra is the 'Double Double' Epsilon Lyrae, seen just to the left (east) of Vega. Those with keen eyesight may resolve the two main fifth magnitude components of Epsilon which lie 207.7″ apart. Binoculars will resolve them easily. When seen through a telescope of 4in (100mm) aperture or more, each component will be seen to be double again, making Epsilon Lyrae a quadruple system. Epsilon$_1$ has components of magnitudes 5.0 and 6.1 lying 2.6″ apart, while the 5.2 and 5.5 magnitude components of Epsilon$_2$ are separated by 2.3″.

ABOVE LEFT: *Finder chart for M56 globular cluster. Gamma Lyrae is shown on p.45.*

ABOVE RIGHT: *Region of Lyra (just below and to left of centre) and part of Draco (Head of Draco visible at top of picture) centred near Vega.*

The quadrilateral of stars seen at the top of the picture forms the head of Draco, the Dragon. The faintest (*top*) star of the four is the double star Nu Draconis, both components of which are equal in brightness at magnitude 4.6. Lying at a distance of 61.9″ apart, the two components of Nu Draconis are easily resolved with binoculars.

Star clusters in the region of Ara and Norma

The two constellations Ara (the Altar) and Norma (the Level) lie across the southern Milky Way and the whole area abounds with open star clusters, a number of which are shown below. NGC 6067, visible immediately to the north of Kappa Normae, is a collection of around 100 stars shining with a combined magnitude of 5.6. Lying at a distance of around 6,500 light-years, NGC 6067 can be partially resolved in binoculars, although small telescopes bring out many individual cluster members. Equally impressive is the open cluster NGC 6087, seen some 4° to the south of NGC 6067. Here we have a group of 40 stars with a combined magnitude of 5.4 lying at a distance of 3,000 light years. As with NGC 6067, this object looks attractive through small telescopes.

NGC 6134 is a marvellous sight in binoculars. Shining with a combined magnitude of 7.2, NGC 6134 lies at a distance of just over 2,500 light-years. Telescopes reveal many pairs of stars scattered across the group. NGC 6152 contains 70 stars scattered over an area of sky 30' across, equal to that of the lunar disc. At magnitude 8, it is well worth seeking out in binoculars.

Ara contains a number of open clusters that are observable through binoculars, including NGC 6193, a magnitude 5.2 object lying at a distance of almost

BELOW: *Open cluster NGC 6152 in Ara.*

BOTTOM: *Chart of Ara and Norma showing location of several open star clusters.*

4,500 light-years. Small telescopes will show many individual stars in the group. IC 4651, visible close to Alpha Arae, is a collection of 80 stars shining with a combined magnitude of 6.9 and located at a distance of some 2,600 light-years. NGC 6253 can be seen just to the north of Epsilon₁ Arae. However, telescopes of 3in (75mm) aperture will be needed to resolve any of the 30 member stars of this magnitude 10.2 object.

Many of the other clusters plotted on this chart can be made out by sweeping the sky with good binoculars or a rich field telescope, and by using the frame-

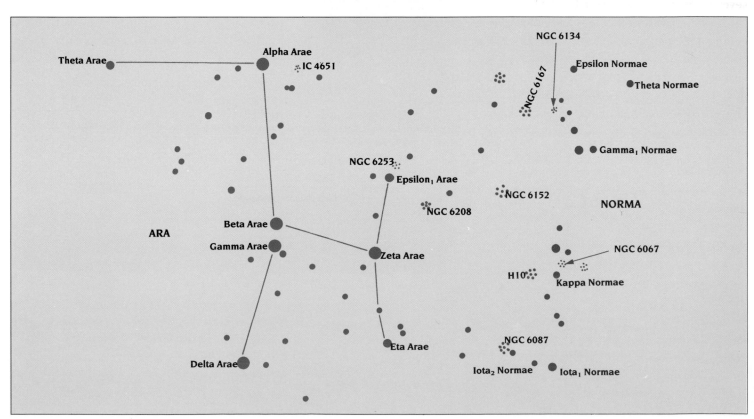

work of stars shown as a guide to your search. As a general rule, large scattered objects require low magnifications and wide fields of view in order that the entire object can be seen in the telescopic field. Smaller objects may repay observation with higher magnifications.

If you have initial difficulty in locating the clusters shown here (or indeed anywhere else in the sky), keep trying. Eventually you will learn to identify objects such as these which may have escaped your attention before. This same basic rule applies to all branches of observation.

Region of sky centred on Norma

The star Gamma$_2$ Normae can be seen here at the centre of the picture below, with the distinctive wedge shape of Norma stretching away above it. Several of the clusters plotted and described on this page can also be made out, notably NGC 6067 seen just above Kappa Normae, the bottom star in the tiny diamond of stars seen roughly halfway between Gamma$_2$ Normae and bottom of picture. NGC 6087 is also prominent immediately to the left of the line of three stars near the bottom margin. The rich starfields of the Milky Way can also be seen running from upper left to lower right of picture. By comparing the photograph with the accompanying chart of Ara and Norma, several more open clusters can be identified.

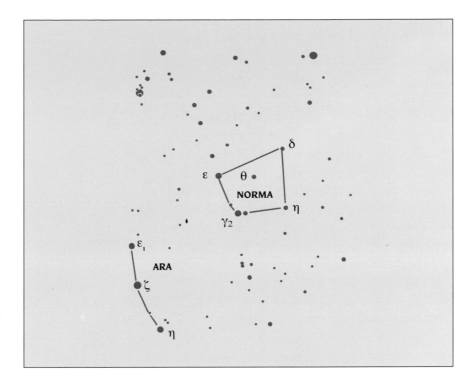

ABOVE: *Identification chart for photograph of region of sky centred on Norma. Chart covers same area as photograph below left.*

BELOW LEFT: *Photograph of region of sky centred on Norma. A chart of this area is given at the top of this page.*

BELOW RIGHT: *Open cluster NGC 6193 in Ara with the emission nebula NGC 6188.*

NGC 6193 and emission nebula NGC 6188

Below we see the open star cluster NGC 6193 in Ara, a young cluster thought to be only a few million years old. Below it (in this picture) is a conspicuous band of dark dust, this material being the remnants of the giant cloud from which the stars in the cluster were formed. Although the cluster seen here is clearly visible in binoculars or a small telescope, the surrounding nebulosity is not. Large telescopes and clear nights are required in order that hints of the nebulosity seen here will be resolved.

DETAILED CHARTS FOR NORTHERN AUTUMN/ SOUTHERN SPRING

Mira

Mira was the first variable star to be discovered and is typical of long period variables in that its maxima and minima are not constant. Mira varies from around magnitude 3 to 9 or 10. On one occasion, in 1779, it almost reached magnitude 1. The period is also subject to variations and averages out at around 331 days. Mira is the brightest and best known of the long period pulsating variables, and only moderate optical equipment is required in order to follow its complete cycle of variability.

The accompanying location and comparison charts will enable you to find Mira. Observation will be impossible during northern spring/southern autumn as Cetus will be in the same region of sky as the Sun, and therefore in the sky during daylight hours. Cetus becomes visible from around August when, during the early hours of the morning, it will be seen in the southeastern sky by observers at mid-northern latitudes. As the year wears on the constellation becomes more and more favourably placed, until it is visible high in the south from mid-northern latitudes during November. For southern hemisphere observers, Cetus is also well placed during November, although at this time it will be seen high in the northern part of

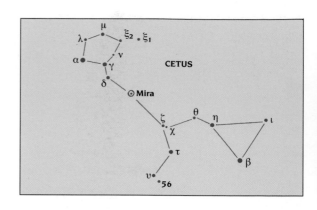

ABOVE: *The stars of Cetus, showing location of Mira.*

BELOW: *Chart of comparison stars for Mira.*

the sky. Cetus finally moves into the daytime sky in January from which time it will be unobservable until the following August.

Once located, estimate the magnitude of Mira in relation to the other stars indicated and whose magnitudes are given in the table below. Although first time or inexperienced observers may have problems estimating its precise magnitude, the fact that it is changing in magnitude will be readily apparent over time. If you have difficulty in picking Mira out, this may be because it is at or near its minimum brightness. If this is the case, repeat your search again over the following month or so until it becomes bright enough to be visible. Once located, observations should be made on a weekly basis. Its complete cycle of variability can be followed by repeated observation during the months that Cetus is visible in the sky.

Mira (Omicron Ceti) Comparison Chart
Long period pulsating variable

Maximum brightness: magnitude 2 or 3
Minimum brightness: magnitude 9 or 10
Period: 331 days on average

COMPARISON STARS

Beta Ceti 2.00	75 Ceti 5.34
Alpha Ceti 2.52	70 Ceti 5.41
Eta Ceti 3.44	G 6.00
Mu Ceti 4.26	71 Ceti 6.40
Xi$_2$ Ceti 4.27	F 6.49
Xi$_1$ Ceti 4.36	A 7.19
Lambda Ceti 4.70	B 8.00
Nu Ceti 4.87	C 8.60
	D 8.80
	E 9.20

Eridanus and Cetus with Mira

This view (right) shows parts of the constellations Cetus and Eridanus with Mira near maximum brightness in January 1978. Mira is the reddish star near the top right corner of picture. The bluish-white star to its upper left, near the top margin, is Delta Ceti, while the stars near lower right margin are the close pair Zeta (top) and Chi Ceti and, below these, Tau Ceti. The large loop of stars occupying the left half of picture lie in Eridanus, although the small quadrilateral just right of centre belongs to Cetus. Many of the brightest stars in this picture can be identified from the chart on page 46.

Pegasus, Andromeda, Triangulum and Aries

For observers in the northern hemisphere, the autumn night sky is dominated by Pegasus and Andromeda. Star charts tend to give the impression that Pegasus, and in particular the four stars that make up the Square of Pegasus, is a prominent group, although the stars concerned are not particularly bright. The Square is situated high above the southern horizon during late evenings in October, and is best placed for observation at this time. It is large and somewhat obscure, and care will be needed if you are seeking it out for the first time. Once located, however, it will easily be found again.

ABOVE: *Parts of Eridanus and Cetus photographed in January 1978 with the long-period variable star Mira (Omicron Ceti) near maximum brightness Mira is the reddish star near the top right (north-west) corner of picture.*

BELOW: *The stars of Pegasus, Andromeda, Triangulum and Aries.*

The four stars that form the Square are Alpha Pegasi, or Markab; Beta Pegasi, or Scheat; Gamma Pegasi, or Algenib and Alpha Andromedae, or Alpheratz, which is 'borrowed' from neighbouring Andromeda. At first sight, the Square seems virtually devoid of stars that can be seen with the naked eye, the only two stars that could be described as prominent being Upsilon and Tau Pegasi. However, given clear skies, around a dozen stars (or even more) can be counted within the confines of the Square.

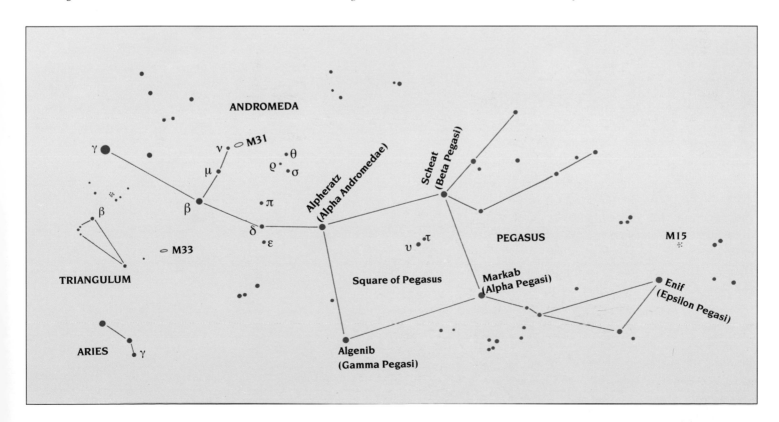

Pegasus is home to the fairly bright globular cluster M15 (NGC 7078), located a little to the north-west of Epsilon Pegasi, or Enif. The accompanying finder chart will help you locate M15 once Enif has been identified. Lying at a distance of over 30,000 light-years, M15 has a magnitude of 6.4 and appears as a fuzzy starlike object in binoculars. However, telescopes of 4in (100mm) aperture or more will help to resolve many of M15's outlying stars. Andromeda contains several objects of interest to the owners of binoculars or small telescopes. The bright star Gamma Andromedae, or Almach, is one of the prettiest doubles in the sky. Its magnitude 2.3 and 5.1 components are separated by 9.4″. Gamma Andromedae offers a beautiful colour contrast between its two member stars which have yellowish-orange and bluish tints.

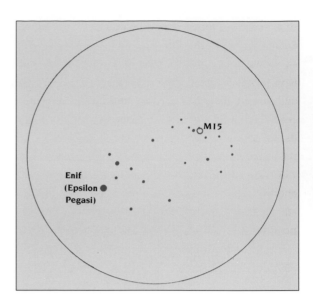

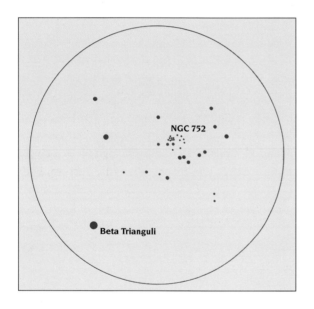

RIGHT: *Finder chart for M15 globular cluster. Epsilon Pegasi is identified on pages 46 and 65.*

LEFT: *Finder chart for NGC 752 open cluster. Beta Trianguli is identified on pages 46 and 65.*

BELOW RIGHT: *Finder chart for M33 spiral galaxy. Alpha Trianguli is identified on pages 46 and 65.*

To the south of Gamma is the open star cluster NGC 752, located by star hopping from Beta Trianguli as shown on the accompanying finder chart. NGC 752 is a fine cluster some 45′ across, roughly one and a half times the size of the lunar disc. Binoculars reveal some of its individual stars, although the best views are obtained with telescopes using low-power eye-pieces. NGC 752 is a fairly scattered collection of stars and is best seen in a wide field of view.

Andromeda plays host to one of the most famous deep sky objects, the Andromeda Galaxy, or M31 (NGC 224). M31 is a spiral galaxy, similar (but larger) than our own and thought to contain in excess of 300 billion stars. Lying at a distance of over two million light-years, it is the largest and brightest member of the Local Group of galaxies, a cluster of some two dozen galaxies of which our own Milky Way Galaxy is also a member.

M31 is visible to the unaided eye as a misty streak of light just to the west of Nu Andromedae. Even binoculars will show that the brightest part of M31 is its core, the spiral arms visible as a much fainter nebulous area spreading out to either side. The total magnitude is around 3.5. The Andromeda Galaxy was referred to as the 'Little Cloud' by the Persian astronomer Al Sufi in the tenth century, a description which holds good today. Its true identity, that of a colossal galaxy containing billions of stars, was not realized until earlier this century. M31 is a truly splendid object and a popular target for the backyard astronomer.

Another member of the Local Group is M33 (NGC 598) in the north-western reaches of the small constellation Triangulum. M33 is a face-on spiral, unlike M31 which is seen almost edge-on from our position in space. It has a very low surface brightness and is extremely difficult to pick out unless the sky is really

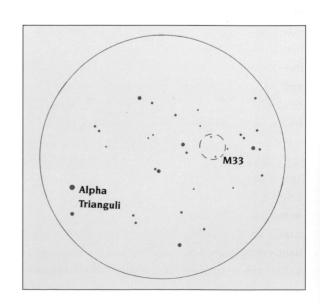

dark and clear. Moonlight will blot it out completely. Search for M33 using the accompanying chart which shows its position relative to Alpha Trianguli. You will have more chance of success if you look for a faint and extensive patch of light rather than a more concentrated light source. Its total magnitude is 5.7 and its surface area covers roughly 60′ × 40′, over twice the apparent size of the full Moon.

A little way to the south of Triangulum is Aries, another small constellation. This is an easy double star for small telescopes. Gamma Arietis has two components, both of magnitude 4.8 separated by 7.8″.

LEFT: *Parts of Andromeda with the stars Beta (lower), Mu and Nu Andromeda visible near the left-hand margin. The Andromeda spiral galaxy (M31) is seen to the immediate upper right (west) of Nu.*

BELOW RIGHT: *Piscus Austrinus and Grus area. Fomalhaut is the bright star visible to the upper left of centre with the 'Lambda' shape of Grus prominent in the lower (southern) hald of the picture.*

Part of Andromeda with M31

This view shows part of Andromeda with the Andromeda Spiral Galaxy clearly visible just to the upper right (west) of Nu Andromedae, the top star in the line of three stars to left of picture. Below it are Mu and Beta Andromedae, while several more of the brightest stars on this photograph can be identified by comparison with the chart on page 65.

Piscis Austrinus and Grus

This photograph (right) shows the region of sky around Piscis Austrinus and Grus. Located between Aquarius to the north and Grus to the south, Piscis Austrinus is a fairly small constellation. Its brightest star is Fomalhaut, easily located by using the Square of Pegasus as a direction finder (see chart on page 46). Piscis Austrinus contains two double stars, observable with small telescopes. One of these is Beta Piscis Austrini, which has magnitude 4.4 and 7.9 components separated by 30.3″. Small telescopes will resolve this pair, although larger instruments will be needed to split the two components of Gamma Piscis Austrini, seen a few degrees to the east of Beta. The two stars forming the Gamma system shine with magnitudes of 4.5 and 8. Their separation is only 4.2″ which, coupled with the appreciable difference in magnitudes, make them difficult to resolve through telescopes of less than 4in (100mm) aperture. Many of the brighter stars, including Fomalhaut (seen to upper left of centre) can be identified from the chart on page 47.

To the south (below) of Piscis Austrinus is the conspicuous form of Grus which, as can be seen, contains a number of wide naked-eye pairs of stars. Of all the heavenly birds that adorn the southern sky, Grus is by far the most impressive. For binocular observers, the two stars Alpha and Beta Gruis (*see* page 46) offer a lovely colour contrast, the bluish-white of Alpha standing out against orangish Beta.

Also visible here, just above a line joining Alpha and Beta and forming a triangle with this pair, is the binocular double formed from the 6th magnitude stars Pi_1 and Pi_2 Gruis, seen in this photograph as a single starlike point. Binoculars will easily resolve both components, while large telescopes will show that each star is double again. The brighter component of Pi_1 is a variable star which fluctuates between magnitudes 5.4 and 6.7 over a period of around 150 days.

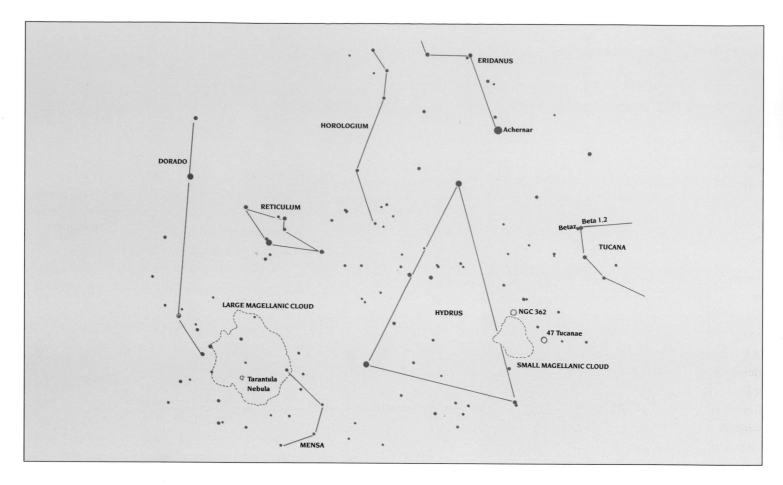

DETAILED CHART FOR SOUTH CIRCUMPOLAR STARS
Chart of Large and Small Magellanic Clouds

The region of sky shown above is occupied by a number of relatively faint constellations. The bright star Achernar, lying at the southern end of Eridanus (the River Eridanus), will act as a guide for picking out one or two of the groups charted.

By far the most impressive objects here are the two irregular galaxies, the Large (LMC) and Small (SMC) Magellanic Clouds. Galaxies are made up mainly of stars, nebulae and interstellar material and there are several different types, including spirals, barred spirals, elliptical and irregular systems. Our own Milky Way is a spiral galaxy, containing spiral arms radiating from a central bulge. In addition to the spirals are the barred spiral galaxies in which the arms emanate from the ends of a bar which crosses the central regions of the system. Elliptical galaxies, which are by far the most numerous type, have a regular, uniform appearance, while irregular galaxies, such as the Magellanic Clouds, have no well-defined shape. These different groups are further sub-divided into different classes. The spirals and barred spirals are classified according

ABOVE: Chart of region around Large and Small Magellanic Clouds.

to how tightly wound are their spiral arms, while the ellipticals are graded according to their exact shape, which can be anything ranging from almost spherical to highly elliptical.

Most galaxies are members of huge collections, or clusters, of galaxies. The Magellanic Clouds are both members of the Local Group of Galaxies, a gathering of two dozen or more galaxies of which our own Milky Way, the Andromeda Spiral and the Triangulum Spiral are the three largest members. Most of the other galaxies within the Local Group are dwarf elliptical systems. Clusters of galaxies can be seen scattered throughout the universe, a well-known example being the Virgo Cluster.

The Magellanic Clouds are both fairly close to us, the LMC lying at a distance of around 160,000 light-years, and the SMC some 200,000 light-years distant. Visually, they take the form of huge nebulous patches, resembling detached portions of the Milky Way. The LMC straddles the borders of the constellations Dorado (the Goldfish) and Mensa (the Table Mountain), while the SMC is situated around 22° away, entirely within the boundaries of Tucana (the Toucan). The actual separation of the two systems is 80,000 light-years.

As with other galaxies, both these objects contain many different types of celestial object including open and globular clusters and nebulae. Careful sweeping with binoculars or a rich-field telescope will reveal a number of examples of each object type. Visible in the same field as the SMC are a pair of fine globular clusters. The fainter of the two, NGC 362, lies just to the north of the SMC, while NGC 104, also known as 47 Tucanae, can be seen roughly 2.5° to the west. Although appearing to be associated with the SMC, both these globulars are actually members of our own Galaxy. 47 Tucanae is indeed one of the closest known globulars, situated at a distance of around 16,000 light-years. Its overall magnitude is around 4, making it easily visible to the unaided eye as a small, nebulous star-like object. Telescopes of 6in (150mm) aperture and upwards will resolve many individual stellar members of 47 Tucanae; it is widely regarded as one of the best globulars in the entire heavens, second only in visual splendour to Omega Centauri. NGC 362, at magnitude 7, hovers on the edge of naked-eye visibility, although some form of optical aid is usually required to see it.

Lying in the same general field as the SMC is the pretty multiple star Beta Tucanae. $Beta_1$ (mag 4.4) and $Beta_2$ (magnitude 4.8) are separated by 27.1″ while $Beta_3$ lies within the same low-power field.

The LMC also contains a wealth of objects visible to the backyard astronomer. Many clusters and nebulae are visible through only moderate optical aid. Of all the objects found within the LMC, pride of place must go to the 5th magnitude Tarantula Nebula (NGC 2070), a truly striking feature comprising a vast cloud of glowing hydrogen which contains many bright, young stars. The Tarantula Nebula is the most complex object of its type known and, with a diameter estimated to be some 800 light years (this value being roughly doubled if its outer streamers and loops are taken into account), it totally dwarfs the Orion Nebula. If it were placed at the same distance as the Orion Nebula, the Tarantula would cover an area of sky around 30° across, and would have dimensions roughly equivalent to the entire constellation of Orion!

THE TARANTULA NEBULA *The brightest of the LMC's showpieces is the Tarantula Nebula (above) which, even at its distance of around 160,000 light-years, glows at around magnitude 5 and is visible to the naked eye.*

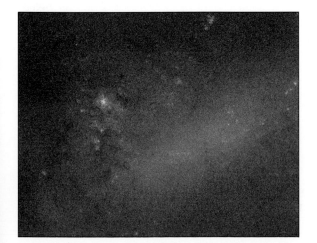

LARGE MAGELLANIC CLOUD: *This close-up view off the LMC (left) shows resolution into many thousands of individual stars. A large number of open star clusters can also be seen, as can the bright knot of nebulosity, the Tarantula Nebula, to the upper left of centre.*

Centaurus, Crux, Musca and Lupus (on page 70)

Although Crux (the Cross) is the smallest of all the constellations, it is also one of the most famous and home to many objects of interest to the backyard astronomer. Its leading star Acrux is a double, its magnitude 1.4 and 1.9 white and blue-white components separated by 4.4″. Both stars can be seen in small telescopes, as can a third star of magnitude 4.9 located 90.1″ away. Another double star is Gamma Crucis which has an orange magnitude 1.6 primary, located 110.6″ away from its magnitude 6.7 white companion. A third star, of magnitude 9.5, lies 155.2″ away from the primary. All three stars can be seen in telescopes of 3in (75mm) aperture.

Another two of Crux's doubles are worth seeking out. Eta Crucis has magnitude 4.2 and 11.7 components lying 44″ apart, although telescopes of around 4in (100mm) aperture will be needed to enable the glow from the fainter component to be seen in the glare of its brighter companion. Iota Crucis has 4.7 and 9.5 magnitude components separated by 26.9″.

The Kappa Crucis open cluster (NGC 4755), popularly known as the Jewel Box, is a splendid object for small telescopes. Resolvable into stars even through

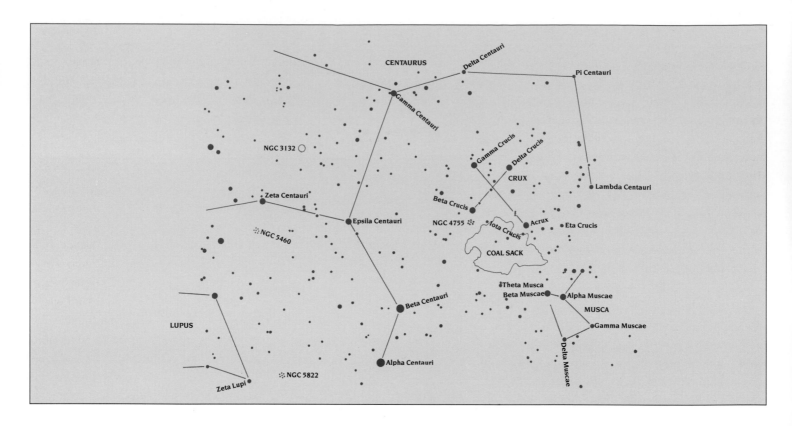

binoculars, the Jewel Box contains a number of very bright stars, some of which have distinct blue and red tints, lending a beautiful splash of colour to this stunning object.

Lying at a distance of around 7,500 light-years, the Jewel Box appears to be located on the northern edge of the Coal Sack dark nebula. However, the association is no more than a line of sight effect, the Coal Sack being located only around 500 light-years away from us. This huge, dark object is a cloud of absorbing dust which blots out the light from the stars beyond. The overall effect is that of a huge hole in the surrounding star fields of the Milky Way.

Immediately to the south of the Crux is the small but conspicuous pattern of stars we call Musca (the Fly). Theta Muscae is a double star resolvable in small telescopes, its magnitude 5.7 and 7.3 yellowish and white components lying 5.3″ apart. Theta Muscae is an attractive sight in small telescopes, particularly so because it lies within a rich field of stars.

Crux is surrounded on three sides by Centaurus (the Centaur), a much larger group and the ninth largest constellation in the sky. Alpha Centauri is an easy double star for small telescopes, its magnitude 0 and 1.2 yellow components separated by 19.7″.

Lying a little way to the south of Zeta Centauri is the magnitude 5.6 open cluster NGC 5460. Containing around 40 stars, NGC 5460 shines from a distance of

OMEGA CENTAURI *The visually stunning globular cluster Omega Centauri, shown below, is widely regarded as the finest globular in the heavens.*

around 1,600 light-years and is easily picked up in binoculars. Small telescopes will resolve one or two of this cluster's member stars.

The magnificent globular cluster Omega Centauri (NGC 5139) is widely regarded as the best example of a globular cluster in the heavens. It is certainly the brightest, and its multitude of stars covers an area of sky roughly equal to that of the full lunar disc. It is found by extending the line from Beta through Epsilon Centauri almost as far again, and is visible to the unaided eye as a nebulous spot. It was recorded almost 2,000 years ago by the Greek astronomer Ptolemy who catalogued it as a star, as did the German astronomer Johann Bayer, who consequently listed it as Omega Centauri in the early seventeenth century. It was not until 1677 that the English astronomer Edmund Halley discovered its true nature. Resolution

into stars is achieved even with binoculars, and telescopes really bring out the splendour of this magnificent object. Omega Centauri lies at a distance of around 17,000 light-years.

Lying on a line from Alpha Centauri to Zeta Lupi is the widely scattered open cluster NGC 5822. Containing around 150 stars, NGC 5822 shines with a magnitude of 6.5 from a distance of some 1,800 light-years. This cluster occupies an area of sky some 40′ across, making it larger than the full lunar disc. Consequently, observation is best carried out either with binoculars or rich-field telescopes, the wide fields of view of which will be needed in order to bring out the full visual effect of this cluster.

scattered along the plane of our Galaxy's disc as seen from Earth. Although most of the stars are too faint to be seen without optical aid, their combined light produces the glow that can often be seen crossing the sky on dark, clear nights. Because we are surrounded by the disc of our Galaxy, the Milky Way is visible in all directions, and forms a band of light right around the celestial sphere.

The Coal Sack dark nebula is prominent in this picture just below Crux, as are the two bright stars Alpha and Beta Centauri near the left margin. At the right of the picture is the prominent glow of the Eta Carinae Nebula. This is a vast cloud of gas surrounding the variable star Eta Carinae, a highly luminous object thought to lie at a distance of around 8,000 light-years. When first catalogued, Eta Carinae was of 3rd magnitude, although it was seen to vary considerably over the following years, reaching magnitude −0.8 in 1843, before sinking to 6th magnitude obscurity by 1868 where it remains today. Material ejected from the star, or from dust clouds around the star, are thought to play a role in the variability of Eta Carinae.

The Eta Carinae Nebula is well worth observing, even with binoculars or small telescopes, as is the magnificent open cluster NGC 3532, seen here just to the upper left of the Eta Carinae Nebula. This magnitude 3.0 object contains around 150 stars and shines from a distance of some 1400 light years. Wide fields of view are essential here as NGC 3532 occupies an area of sky 55′ across, almost twice the diameter of the full Moon.

ALPHA AND BETA CENTAURI AND CRUX: *Here we see the conspicuous form of Crux a little way above the centre of the picture (left), with two bright stars Alpha and Beta Centauri prominent to their left. Musca is clearly visible a little to the lower left of Crux.*

CRUX AND THE COAL SACK DARK NEBULA *In the photograph (below left), the constellation Crux is seen together with the conspicuous form of the Coal Sack dark nebula. The Jewel Box open cluster is visible just above (to the north) of the Coal Sack, just to the lower left of Beta Crucis.*

Milky Way running through Crux
We see the Milky Way running through the region of Crux, visible at the centre of the picture at right. The Milky Way is created by the combined glow of stars,

Appendices

GUIDE TO LIST OF CONSTELLATIONS

Name: The name of the constellation. An asterisk (*) denotes that the constellation was in the list of 48 groups drawn up by the Greek astronomer Ptolemy, almost 2,000 years ago. In all, Ptolemy listed 21 northern groups, 12 Zodiacal and 15 southern. In addition to those indicated was Argo Navis (the Ship Argo). This group was somewhat large and unwieldy, and has since been broken up into three separate constellations – Carina (the Keel), Vela (the Sails) and Puppis (the Stern) – thereby at least keeping the nautical traditions intact!

The constellation Serpens (the Serpent) is actually divided into two parts, known individually as Serpens Caput (the Head of the Serpent) and Serpens Cauda (the Tail of the Serpent). The group which divides Serpens is (appropriately) Ophiuchus (the Serpent-

Bearer), a constellation formerly known as Serpentarius. In spite of the division, Serpens is classed as a single group.

Abbr: The abbreviated form of the constellation name.

Genitive form: The genitive form of the constellation name. For details of its use in star identification, see 'What's In A Name'?

Meaning: Translation of the constellation name.

Area: The area of the constellation in square degrees.

Order of size: Ranking of the constellation in order of area, ranging from the largest group (Hydra – 1303 sq deg) down to the smallest (Crux – 68 sq deg).

Bright stars: List of stars of magnitude 2 or brighter.

Greek alphabet

Αα	Alpha
Ββ	Beta
Γγ	Gamma
Δδ	Delta
Εε	Epsilon
Ζζ	Zeta
Ηη	Eta
Θθ	Theta
Ιι	Iota
Κκ	Kappa
Λλ	Lambda
Μμ	Mu
Νν	Nu
Ξξ	Xi or Si
Οο	Omicron
Ππ	Pi
Ρϱ	Rho
Σσζ	Sigma
Ττ	Tau
Υυ	Upsilon
Φφ	Phi
Χχ	Chi
Ψψ	Psi
Ωω	Omega

The Brightest Stars

NAME	CONSTELLATION	APPARENT MAGNITUDE	ABSOLUTE MAGNITUDE	DISTANCE (L.Y.)
Sirius	Canis Major	−1·42	+1·4	8·7
Canopus	Carina	−0·72	−8·5	1170
Alpha Centauri	Centaurus	−0·27	+4·4	4·43
Arcturus	Bootes	−0·06	−0·2	37
Vega	Lyra	+0·04	+0·5	27
Capella	Auriga	0·06	−0·3	45
Rigel	Orion	0·14	−7·1	900
Procyon	Canis Minor	0·35	+2·6	11·3
Achernar	Eridanus	0·53	−1·6	120
Hadar	Centaurus	0·66	−5·1	490
Betelgeuse	Orion	0·70 (v)	−5·6 (v)	520
Altair	Aquila	0·77	+2·2	16
Aldebaran	Taurus	0·86	−0·3	68
Acrux	Crux	0·87	−3·9	370
Antares	Scorpius	0·92 (v)	−4·7 (v)	520
Spica	Virgo	1·00 (v)	−3·5 (v)	275
Pollux	Gemini	1·16	+0·2	35
Fomalhaut	Pisces Austrinus	1·17	+2·0	23
Deneb	Cygnus	1·26	−7·5	1600
Beta Crucis	Crux	1·28	−4·6	490

(v) denotes star is variable

List of Constellations

NAME		ABBR	GENITIVE FORM	MEANING	AREA	ORDER OF SIZE	BRIGHT STARS
Andromeda	★	And	Andromedae	Andromeda	722	19	
Antlia		Ant	Antliae	The Air Pump	239	62	
Apus		Aps	Apodis	The Bird of Paradise	206	67	
Aquarius	★	Aqr	Aquarii	The Water Carrier	980	10	
Aquila	★	Aql	Aquilae	The Eagle	652	22	Altair
Ara	★	Ara	Arae	The Altar	237	63	
Aries	★	Ari	Arietis	The Ram	441	39	Hamal
Auriga	★	Aur	Aurigae	The Charioteer	657	21	Capella, Menkalinan
Boötes	★	Boo	Boötis	The Herdsman	907	13	Arcturus
Caelum		Cae	Caeli	The Graving Tool	125	81	
Camelopardalis		Cam	Camelopardalis	The Giraffe	757	18	
Cancer	★	Cnc	Cancri	The Crab	506	31	
Canes Venatici		CVn	Canum Venaticorum	The Hunting Dogs	465	38	
Canis Major	★	CMa	Canis Majoris	The Great Dog	380	43	Sirius, Adhara, Wezen, Mirzam
Canis Minor	★	CMi	Canis Minoris	The Little Dog	183	71	Procyon
Capricornus	★	Cap	Capricorni	The Goat	414	40	
Carina		Car	Carinae	The Keel	494	34	Canopus, Miaplacidus, Avior
Cassiopeia	★	Cas	Cassiopeiae	Cassiopeia	598	25	
Centaurus	★	Cen	Centauri	The Centaur	1060	9	Alpha Centauri, Hadar
Cepheus	★	Cep	Cephei	Cepheus	588	27	
Cetus	★	Cet	Ceti	The Whale	1231	4	
Chamaeleon		Cha	Chamaeleonis	The Chameleon	132	79	
Circinus		Cir	Circini	The Pair of Compasses	93	85	
Columba		Col	Columbae	The Dove	270	54	
Coma Berenices		Com	Comae Berenicis	Berenice's Hair	386	42	
Corona Australis	★	CrA	Coronae Australis	The Southern Crown	128	80	
Corona Borealis	★	CrB	Coronae Borealis	The Northern Crown	179	73	
Corvus	★	Crv	Corvi	The Crow	184	70	
Crater	★	Crt	Crateris	The Cup	282	53	
Crux		Cru	Crucis	The Cross	68	88	Acrux, Beta Crucis, Gamma Crucis
Cygnus	★	Cyg	Cygni	The Swan	804	16	Deneb
Delphinus	★	Del	Delphini	The Dolphin	189	69	
Dorado		Dor	Doradus	The Goldfish	179	72	
Draco	★	Dra	Draconis	The Dragon	1083	8	
Equuleus	★	Equ	Equulei	The Foal	72	87	
Eridanus	★	Eri	Eridani	The River Eridanus	1138	6	Achernar
Fornax		For	Fornacis	The Furnace	398	41	
Gemini	★	Gem	Geminorum	The Twins	514	30	Pollux, Castor, Alhena
Grus		Gru	Gruis	The Crane	366	45	Alnair
Hercules	★	Her	Herculis	Hercules	1225	5	
Horologium		Hor	Horologii	The Pendulum Clock	249	58	
Hydra	★	Hya	Hydrae	The Water Snake	1303	1	Alfard
Hydrus		Hyi	Hydri	The Little Water Snake	243	61	
Indus		Ind	Indi	The Indian	294	49	
Lacerta		Lac	Lacertae	The Lizard	201	68	
Leo	★	Leo	Leonis	The Lion	947	12	Regulus, Algieba
Leo Minor		LMi	Leonis Minoris	The Little Lion	232	64	
Lepus	★	Lep	Leporis	The Hare	290	51	

List of Constellations

NAME		ABBR	GENITIVE FORM	MEANING	AREA	ORDER OF SIZE	BRIGHT STARS
Libra	★	Lib	Librae	The Scales	538	29	
Lupus	★	Lup	Lupi	The Wolf	334	46	
Lynx		Lyn	Lyncis	The Lynx	545	28	
Lyra	★	Lyr	Lyrae	The Lyre	286	52	Vega
Mensa		Men	Mensae	The Table Mountain	153	75	
Microscopium		Mic	Microscopii	The Microscope	210	66	
Monoceros		Mon	Monocerotis	The Unicorn	482	35	
Musca		Mus	Muscae	The Fly	138	77	
Norma		Nor	Normae	The Level	165	74	
Octans		Oct	Octantis	The Octant	291	50	
Ophiuchus	★	Oph	Ophiuchi	The Serpent-Bearer	948	11	
Orion	★	Ori	Orionis	Orion	594	26	Rigel, Betelgeuse, Bellatrix, Alnilam, Alnitak
Pavo		Pav	Pavonis	The Peacock	378	44	Alpha Pavonis
Pegasus	★	Peg	Pegasi	Pegasus	1121	7	
Perseus	★	Per	Persei	Perseus	615	24	Mirfak
Phoenix		Phe	Phoenicis	The Phoenix	469	37	
Pictor		Pic	Pictoris	The Painter's Easel	247	59	
Pisces	★	Psc	Piscium	The Fishes	889	14	
Piscis Austrinus	★	PsA	Piscis Austrini	The Southern Fish	245	60	Fomalhaut
Puppis		Pup	Puppis	The Stern	673	20	
Pyxis		Pyx	Pyxidis	The Mariner's Compass	221	65	
Reticulum		Ret	Reticuli	The Net	114	82	
Sagitta	★	Sge	Sagittae	The Arrow	80	86	
Sagittarius	★	Sgr	Sagittarii	The Archer	867	15	Kaus Australis
Scorpius	★	Sco	Scorpii	The Scorpion	497	33	Antares, Shaula, Sargas
Sculptor		Scl	Sculptoris	The Sculptor	475	36	
Scutum		Sct	Scuti	The Shield	109	84	
Serpens Caput Serpens Cauda	★	Ser	Serpentis	The Serpent	637	23	
Sextans		Sex	Sextantis	The Sextant	314	47	
Taurus	★	Tau	Tauri	The Bull	797	17	Aldebaran, El Nath
Telescopium		Tel	Telescopii	The Telescope	252	57	
Triangulum	★	Tri	Trianguli	The Triangle	132	78	
Triangulum Australe		TrA	Trianguli Australis	The Southern Triangle	110	83	Atria
Tucana		Tuc	Tucanae	The Toucan	295	48	
Ursa Major	★	UMa	Ursae Majoris	The Great Bear	1280	3	Alioth, Dubhe, Benetnash
Ursa Minor	★	UMi	Ursae Minoris	The Little Bear	256	56	Polaris
Vela		Vel	Velorum	The Sail	500	32	Suhail, Delta Velorum
Virgo	★	Vir	Virginis	The Virgin	1294	2	Spica
Volans		Vol	Volantis	The Flying Fish	141	76	
Vulpecula		Vul	Vulpeculae	The Fox	268	55	

The Nearest Stars

NAME		CONSTELLATION	APPARENT MAGNITUDE	DISTANCE (L.Y.)
Proxima Centauri		Centaurus	+10·7	4·3
Alpha Centauri	★	Centaurus	− 0·27	4·34
Barnard's Star		Ophiuchus	+ 9·5	6·0
Wolf 359		Leo	+13·6	7·7
Lalande 21185		Ursa Major	+ 7·6	8·3
Sirius	★	Canis Major	− 1·42	8·7
Luyten 726–8	★	Cetus	+12·3	9·0
Ross 154		Sagittarius	+10·6	9·5
Ross 248		Andromeda	+12·2	10·3
Epsilon Eridani		Eridanus	+ 3·7	10·8
Luyten 789–6		Aquarius	+12·2	10·8
Ross 128		Virgo	+11·1	10·9
61 Cygni	★	Cygnus	+ 5·2	11·1
Procyon	★	Canis Minor	+ 0·35	11·3
Epsilon Indi		Indus	+ 4·7	11·4
Sigma 2398	★	Draco	+ 8·8	11·4
Groombridge 34	★	Andromeda	+ 8·0	11·7
Tau Ceti		Cetus	+ 3·5	11·8
Lacaille 9352		Pisces Austrinus	+ 7·4	11·9
BD+5°1668		Canis Minor	+ 9·8	12·3

★ denotes star has a companion

The Messier Catalogue

MNo	NGC	R.A. hr mn	DECL ° '	CONSTELLATION	TYPE OF OBJECT	POPULAR NAME
1	1952	05 34.5	+22 01	Taurus	Supernova remnant	Crab Nebula
2	7089	21 33.5	−00 49	Aquarius	Globular	
3	5272	13 42.2	+28 23	Canes Venatici	Globular	
4	6121	16 23.6	−26 32	Scorpius	Globular	
5	5904	15 18.6	+02 05	Serpens	Globular	
6	6405	17 40.1	−32 13	Scorpius	Open cluster	Butterfly Cluster
7	6475	17 53.9	−34 49	Scorpius	Open cluster	
8	6523	18 03.8	−24 23	Sagittarius	Nebula	Lagoon Nebula
9	6333	17 19.2	−18 31	Ophiuchus	Globular	
10	6254	16 57.1	−04 06	Ophiuchus	Globular	
11	6705	18 51.1	−06 16	Scutum	Open Cluster	Wild Duck Cluster
12	6218	16 47.2	−01 57	Ophiuchus	Globular	
13	6205	16 41.7	+36 28	Hercules	Globular	Great Hercules Cluster
14	6402	17 37.6	−03 15	Ophiuchus	Globular	
15	7078	21 30.0	+12 10	Pegasus	Globular	
16	6611	18 18.8	−13 47	Serpens	Nebula and associated cluster	Eagle Nebula
17	6618	18 20.8	−16 11	Sagittarius	Nebula	Omega or Horseshoe Nebula
18	6613	18 19.9	−17 08	Sagittarius	Open cluster	
19	6273	17 02.6	−26 16	Ophiuchus	Globular	
20	6514	18 02.6	−23 02	Sagittarius	Nebula	Trifid Nebula
21	6531	18 04.6	−22 30	Sagittarius	Open cluster	

MNo	NGC	R.A. hr mn	DECL ° '	CONSTELLATION	TYPE OF OBJECT	POPULAR NAME
22	6656	18 36.4	−23 54	Sagittarius	Globular	
23	6494	17 56.8	−19 01	Sagittarius	Open cluster	
24	6603	18 18.4	−18 25	Sagittarius	Star-cloud in Milky Way	
25	14725	18 31.6	−19 15	Sagittarius	Open cluster	
26	6694	18 45.2	−09 24	Scutum	Open cluster	
27	6853	19 59.6	+22 43	Vulpecula	Planetary nebula	Dumbbell Nebula
28	6626	18 24.5	−24 52	Sagittarius	Globular	
29	6913	20 23.9	+38 32	Cygnus	Open cluster	
30	7099	21 40.4	−23 11	Capricornus	Globular	
31	224	00 42.7	+41 16	Andromeda	Spiral galaxy	Great Spiral
32	221	00 42.7	+40 52	Andromeda	Elliptical galaxy	Companion to M31
33	598	01 33.9	+30 39	Triangulum	Spiral galaxy	Triangulum Spiral
34	1039	02 42.0	+42 47	Perseus	Open cluster	
35	2168	06 08.9	+24 20	Gemini	Open cluster	
36	1960	05 36.1	+34 08	Auriga	Open cluster	
37	2099	05 52.4	+32 33	Auriga	Open cluster	
38	1912	05 28.7	+35 50	Auriga	Open cluster	
39	7092	21 32.2	+48 26	Cygnus	Open cluster	
40	–	12 22.4	+58 05	Ursa Major	Double star Winnecke 4; mags 9.0/9.6; sep 50″	
41	2287	06 47.0	−20 44	Canis Major	Open cluster	
42	1976	05 35.4	−05 27	Orion	Nebula	Great Orion Nebula
43	1982	05 35.6	−05 16	Orion	Nebula	Part of M42
44	2632	08 40.1	+19 59	Cancer	Open cluster	Praesepe
45	–	03 47.0	+24 07	Taurus	Open cluster	Pleiades
46	2437	07 41.8	−14 49	Puppis	Open cluster	
47	2422	07 36.6	−14 30	Puppis	Open cluster	
48	2548	08 13.8	−05 48	Hydra	Open cluster	
49	4472	12 29.8	+08 00	Virgo	Elliptical galaxy	
50	2323	07 03.2	−08 20	Monoceros	Open cluster	
51	5194	13 29.9	+47 12	Canes Venatici	Spiral galaxy	Whirlpool Galaxy
52	7654	23 24.2	+61 35	Cassiopeia	Open cluster	
53	5024	13 12.9	+18 10	Coma Berenices	Globular	
54	6715	18 55.1	−30 29	Sagittarius	Globular	
55	6809	19 40.0	−30 58	Sagittarius	Globular	
56	6779	19 16.6	+30 11	Lyra	Globular	
57	6720	18 53.6	+33 02	Lyra	Planetary nebula	Ring Nebula
58	4579	12 37.7	+11 49	Virgo	Spiral galaxy	
59	4621	12 42.0	+11 39	Virgo	Elliptical galaxy	
60	4649	12 43.7	+11 33	Virgo	Elliptical galaxy	
61	4303	12 21.9	+04 28	Virgo	Spiral galaxy	
62	6266	17 01.2	−30 07	Ophiuchus	Globular	
63	5055	13 15.8	+42 02	Canes Venatici	Spiral galaxy	
64	4826	12 56.7	+21 41	Coma Berenices	Spiral galaxy	Black-Eye Galaxy
65	3623	11 18.9	+13 05	Leo	Spiral galaxy	
66	3627	11 20.2	+12 59	Leo	Spiral galaxy	
67	2682	08 50.4	+11 49	Cancer	Open cluster	
68	4590	12 39.5	−26 45	Hydra	Globular	
69	6637	18 31.4	−32 21	Sagittarius	Globular	

MNo	NGC	R.A. hr mn	DECL ° '	CONSTELLATION	TYPE OF OBJECT	POPULAR NAME
70	6681	18 43.2	−32 18	Sagittarius	Globular	
71	6838	19 53.8	+18 47	Sagitta	Globular	
72	6981	20 53.5	−12 32	Aquarius	Globular	
73	6994	20 58.9	−12 38	Aquarius	Asterism of 4 faint stars	
74	628	01 36.7	+15 47	Pisces	Spiral galaxy	
75	6864	20 06.1	−21 55	Sagittarius	Globular	
76	650	01 42.4	+51 34	Perseus	Planetary nebula	Little Dumbbell
77	1068	02 42.7	−00 01	Cetus	Spiral galaxy	
78	2068	05 46.7	+00 03	Orion	Nebula	
79	1904	05 24.5	−24 33	Lepus	Globular	
80	6093	16 17.0	−22 59	Scorpius	Globular	
81	3031	09 55.6	+69 04	Ursa Major	Spiral galaxy	
82	3034	09 55.8	+69 41	Ursa Major	Irregular galaxy	
83	5236	13 37.0	−29 52	Hydra	Spiral galaxy	
84	4374	12 25.1	+12 53	Virgo	Spiral galaxy	
85	4382	12 25.4	+18 11	Coma Berenices	Spiral galaxy	
86	4406	12 26.2	+12 57	Virgo	Elliptical galaxy	
87	4486	12 30.8	+12 24	Virgo	Elliptical galaxy	
88	4501	12 32.0	+14 25	Coma Berenices	Spiral galaxy	
89	4552	12 35.7	+12 33	Virgo	Elliptical galaxy	
90	4569	12 36.8	+13 10	Virgo	Spiral galaxy	
91	4548	12 35.4	+14 30	Coma Berenices	Spiral galaxy	
92	6341	17 17.1	+43 08	Hercules	Globular	
93	2447	07 44.6	−23 52	Puppis	Open cluster	
94	4736	12 50.9	+41 07	Canes Venatici	Spiral galaxy	
95	3351	10 44.0	+11 42	Leo	Barred spiral galaxy	
96	3368	10 46.8	+11 49	Leo	Spiral galaxy	
97	3587	11 14.8	+55 01	Ursa Major	Planetary nebula	Owl Nebula
98	4192	12 13.8	+14 54	Coma Berenices	Spiral galaxy	
99	4254	12 18.8	+14 25	Coma Berenices	Spiral galaxy	
100	4321	12 22.9	+15 49	Coma Berenices	Spiral galaxy	
101	5457	14 03.2	+54 21	Ursa Major	Spiral galaxy	Pinwheel Galaxy
102					Duplicated observation of M101	
103	581	01 33.2	+60 42	Cassiopeia	Open cluster	
104	4594	12 40.0	−11 37	Virgo	Spiral galaxy	Sombrero Hat Galaxy
105	3379	10 47.8	+12 35	Leo	Elliptical galaxy	
106	4258	12 19.0	+47 18	Ursa Major	Spiral galaxy	
107	6171	16 32.5	−13 03	Ophiuchus	Globular	
108	3556	11 11.5	+55 40	Ursa Major	Spiral galaxy	
109	3992	11 57.6	+53 23	Ursa Major	Spiral galaxy	
110	205	00 40.4	+41 41	Andromeda	Elliptical galaxy	Companion to M31

The last object in Messier's original catalogue was M103, the remaining objects all being added in more recent times. M104 was included by Camille Flamarion in 1921 after he discovered a note about the object in Messier's original observing notes. Then came M105, 106 and 107, these additions having been suggested by Helen Sawyer Hogg. M108 and 109 were added by Owen Gingerich after which Kenneth Glyn Jones rounded off the Catalogue with M110 (NGC 205), an object that was actually observed by Messier in 1773 and included on his drawing of M31 published in 1807.

Table of Planetary Data

PLANET	DIAMETER (km)	DISTANCE FROM SUN (km)	SIDEREAL PERIOD (Year)	AXIAL ROTATION PERIOD (Equatorial)	NUMBER OF SATELLITES	MASS (Earth = 1)	MAXIMUM MAGNITUDE
Mercury	4,880	58,000,000	87·97 days	58·65 days	0	0·056	− 1·9
Venus	12,104	108,000,000	224·7 days	243·01 days	0	0·815	− 4·4
Earth	12,756	149,600,000	365·265 days	23·93 hours	1	1·000	−
Mars	6,796	227,900,000	686·98 days	24h 37m 23s	2	0·107	− 2·8
Jupiter	143,800	778,300,000	11·86 years	9h 50m 30s	16	317·89	− 2·6
Saturn	120,660	1,427,000,000	29·46 years	10h 13m 59s	21	95·15	− 0·3
Uranus	50,800	2,870,000,000	84·01 years	17h 14m	15	14·54	+ 5·6
Neptune	49,500	4,497,000,000	164·79 years	17h 50m	8	17·23	+ 7·7
Pluto	2,300	5,900,000,000	248 years	6·3874 days	1	0·002	+14

Useful Addresses

British Astronomical Association
Burlington House
Piccadilly
London WIV 9AG
England

Junior Astronomical Society
36 Fairway
Keyworth
Nottingham NG12 5DU
England

Irish Astronomical Association
The Planetarium
Armagh BT61 9DE
Northern Ireland

British Astronomical Association
New South Wales Branch
P O Box 103
Harbord New South Wales 2096
Australia

American Astronomical Society
2000 Florida Avenue NW
Suite 300
Washington DC 20009
United States of America

Oriental Astronomical Association
c/o Yamamoto Observatory
289 Kamitanakami-Kiryutyo otu
Sigaken 520–21
Japan

Astronomical Society of South Africa
South African Astronomical
   Observatory
P.O. Box 9
Observatory 7935
South Africa

Royal Astronomical Society
   of New Zealand
P.O. Box 3181
Wellington
New Zealand

Royal Astronomical Society of Canada
McLaughlin Planetarium
100 Queens Park
Toronto, Ontario
Canada M5S 2C6

American Association of Variable
   Star Observers
25 Birch Street
Cambridge MA 02138
United States of America

In addition to the above there are many local astronomical societies scattered throughout the world. In many cases their addresses may be available from one of the organizations listed here. A more or less complete listing of local societies worldwide is given in the International Directory of Astronomical Associations and Societies (A. Heck & J. Manfroid), details of price and availability of which are available from:

Centre de Données de Strasbourg
Observatoire Astronomique
11 Rue de l'Université
F–67000 Strasbourg
France

Index

Picture Credits

Key: l=left; r=right; t=top; b=bottom; c=centre

Bernard Abrams/Starland Picture Library: 7b, 11l, 22, 26tr, 26bl, 48b, 51t, 52b, 57b, 60br. Derek Aspinall/Starland Picture Library: 54t, 54b, 55, 56c, 56b, 59tl. Vanessa-Maree Aspinall/ Starland Picture Library: 20, 28, 29t, 29b, 30, 31, 34, 35t, 38, 42, 43, 44, 45, 46, 47, 48t, 49tr, 50t, 50b, 52t, 53, 56t, 57t, 58t, 58b, 59tr, 59b, 60t, 60bl, 61l, 62b, 63t, 64t, 64b, 65b, 66t, 66c, 68, 70t. David Early/FAS/Starland Picture Library: 6. ESO/ Starland Picture Library: 18t, 35b, 37b, 69t, 69b. John Fletcher/ Starland Picture Library: 37t, 49tl. Chris Floyd/Starland Picture Library: 7t, 62t, 63bl, 63br, 67r, 70b, 71bl, 71br. Hale Observatories/Starland Picture Library: 21t, 21b. John Lardlaw/FAS/Starland Picture Library: 71t. Kim Lindley/FAS/ Starland Picture Library: 27b. Raymond Livori/FAS/Starland Picture Library: 65t. Paul L. Money/Starland Picture Library: 9t, 49b. NASA/Starland Picture Library: 12t, 13t, 13b, 14t, 15t, 15b, 16tl, 16tr, 17l, 17r, 18b. National Optical Astronomy/ Observatories/Starland Picture Library: 10. Michael Pace/FAS/ Starland Picture Library: 9b. Geoff Pearce/FAS/Starland Picture Library: 27t, 39t, 39b, 61r, 67l. Ken Phillips/FAS/Starland Picture Library: 51b. Andrew Sefton/FAS/Starland Picture Library: 19. David Strange/FAS/Starland Picture Library: 11r. Anthony Thomas/FAS/Starland Picture Library: 33. Bob Tufnell/FAS/ Starland Picture Library: 14c. Fred Watkins/Starland Picture Library: 23t, 23b, 24, 25l, 25r. Yerkes Observatory/Starland Picture Library: 12b, 40.